Adventures with Ambien and Other Stories

Lin Laurie

Copyright © 2011 Lin Laurie

All rights reserved.

ISBN-10: 1463583362

ISBN-13: 978-1463583361

Dedication

This book is dedicated to my parents with
all my love...

Contents

Introduction	1
My Mother, My Self	3
The Rooster	7
My Mother and a Mirror	9
Hunting for Dinner	10
Hair Brushes & Emotional Hand Grenades	11
Dead Mother in a Corner of the Room	13
Stuttering	15
The Brothers	16
Family Life	20
A Little Parental History	25
Cat Lover	28
Boys and Men	29
The Uninvited One	31
Lack of Understanding	32
Internal Bleeding	39
Paralysis	40
Learning to Fight	43
I Have Seen Magic	46
Boys and Men Revisited	48
Life is a Carnival Old Friend	51
High School Blues	53
Popular Girls	56
Best Friends and Brain Surgeons	58
One Different Thing	62
Minor in the Class	64
Bridge Issues	65
Closing a Business	70
Defending a Name	70
How to Write a Book in Thirty Days	72
Adventures of the Orange Red Lipstick	73
My Neighbor was Probably a Serial Killer	78
Dead Fred	81

Bundles of Boobs	84
The Aftermath…	89
Thank You Ford Motors	90
Running Away	92
Sticking Up for the Underdog	95
The Eighth Brother	96
Gaining Power	98
Psychosomatic 101	99
Running Away Through Life	100
Reality TV vs. Reality Life	107
Breaking Bonaduce	107
Celebrity Rehab with Dr. Drew	108
Being Still	111
I Forgot My Boyfriend's Name	114
Sweet Revenge	117
Stuff Can Make You Crazy	120
Urban Rules of Etiquette	122
Bullies	124
Character Flaws	127
Watermelon Seeds	128
Watermelon Seeds Revisited	129
If Life is a Highway…	129
Perception	131
Calling on People	133
Being Invisible	134
Secrets and Lies	136
Affairs of the Heart	137
Hogzilla!	139
Why Do People Do This?	143
Walk Softly and Don't Use the Phone	146
In Between the Lines	149
Contact List Mania	151
Adventures with Ambien	158
Inspirational Women	165

Adventures with Ambien and Other Stories

Other Writings	167
Manspeak	171
I'm Not Crazy, Just Creative	174
Epilog	181
About the Author	182

Lin Laurie

Adventures with Ambien and Other Stories

Acknowledgments

I want to acknowledge everyone who ever took the time to help me understand the meaning of life.

Lin Laurie

Adventures with Ambien and Other Stories

Introduction

Life is made up of special moments and then you die. To me, the interesting part of life is learning what to make of these moments so that they don't continue on like an echo, reverberating to affect the rest of your life.

This book contains stories of my life and then the meaning that I gave the story of what happened. Some of them are about my parents; others are about my brothers. Later in the book, I talk about things I did as an adult after growing up in such a chaotic environment. My approach to everything is humor; I tell funny stories, I live a fun life, and I intend to die a humorous death doing something unconventional and memorable. I am even open to being caught for eternity doing something very undignified as long as I'm having a good time doing it.

I wrote this book to entertain you with my eccentric, quirky stories; inspire you to persevere in the face of overwhelming situations; and to make you laugh at the craziness of another's family life. I also hope to help you know that as weird and wonderful as your own family life might be, mine is weirder yet, and still, we all love each other very much.

Please enjoy the stories!

Lin Laurie, June 8, 2011

Adventures with Ambien and Other Stories

My Mother, My Self

It is a human trait to try to find evidence in support of the things you believe. We are evidence collecting, reason making, reaffirming-our-actions machines that happen to be called human beings.

The first time I actually had evidence that my mother was different from the other mothers in the neighborhood was the day that I walked in the front door to see an empty six by three picture frame sitting above our dining room table. The picture had been cut out; I recall that it had been some kind of sunny day, flowery meadow with mountains in the background happy kind of image. On this day only a brown backing remained and my mother had stapled weeds, flowers, and other objects to the background.

If it had actually been completely covered with vegetation, it may have had a certain charm to it, but the vegetation was sparse and spread out all over the surface.

It looked crazy. It smelled crazy. It was crazy.

"Mom, what the heck is this?" I whined.

"I wanted to do something different."

"It is different. That's just ugly. Where's our picture?"

Lin Laurie

I was fourteen and I needed normal behavior in my home since there was so little of it anywhere I looked. I came from a large family and was the oldest and only girl in a family that included seven brothers. Just by the numbers we were an unusual family.

"This is much better." My mother replied.

"No it isn't." I was appalled as a fourteen year old could be.

"It's very natural."

"No it isn't. This is not normal!" I shouted at her.

I was so upset. Every day I eyed that damned picture and hoped it would return to its former sunny state. I never wanted to have friends over to see it. I was embarrassed. I did not need my mother to hang something on the wall that would call further attention to the fact that we were a weird bunch. I wanted to fit in. I didn't see that I could never fit in. Our family was too different and we didn't have training in normalcy.

The weeds dried up. The flowers died. I know I said something about it every day it was up there. One day I came home and the picture was gone—so was my mother. It turned out that she had been suffering from postpartum depression, although they didn't call it that in those days. My mother had taken too many pills and had been relocated to the loony bin.

I remember a song on the radio around that time, "They're coming to take me away, ha ha, ho ho..." The men in the white suits had shown up and nabbed my mother.

If I had been embarrassed about the picture, I was mortified by her stay in the loony bin. What do you say to someone when you visit them in there? You aren't supposed to ask things like *why did you want to kill yourself*? *Were you trying to get away from me*? At my age, you take everything personally. Now that I'm older I can understand why having eight children to deal with every day could be a little overwhelming and why a quiet vacation away from them would be something to crave. After all, I retreated to my own bedroom every day to escape them. I retreated into books and imagination to get away from them. But at fourteen you don't see things from that perspective.

So my mother was a nutter. This was something more that I had to endure. I had to take care of my brothers and cook and clean and on and on and on...

During the time my mother was locked up, she convinced me to gather up all her medications, put them in a shoe box, and bring them with me on my next visit to the bin. An orderly found her overdosing under the bed. She had to have her stomach pumped and I had to be told not to do anything she said without running it by my stepfather. I almost caused my mother's death. Oh boy, was I getting ready for some full-on guilt over that situation.

My mother was in the bin for thirty days. She wasn't cured exactly. Her insurance ran out so they sent her home with a big bottle of tranquilizers. It took her a long time to come back to being her old, weird but not depressed self. She was thirty-one years old at the time.

I used to hold my breath and hope that madness and depression were not inherited. I had heard they were and I was sure I'd be taken away by the men in the white coats if I exhibited any odd behavior. I continued to believe this up until I was thirty-two. Then I figuratively exhaled and began to live my own crazy, creative life without any fear that I was bonkers. The idea of like mother, like daughter ceased to have much power over me at that point. I just gave it up.

But until then, I knew I was crazy; it ran in the family. My mother must not love me if she was willing to kill herself and leave me knowing that I had given her the pills to help her do it. I cannot tell you how many years of therapy I needed to recover from her actions.

The Rooster

My grandfather lived with us for several years in a small, four bedroom home in suburban Fremont, California. He was an old farmer and he insisted on bringing his prize rooster with him when he moved in.

This rooster was called Barney and he was very loud and extremely reliable. He never missed his morning wakeup session, up before the crack of dawn, perched high on the fence that separated us from our neighbors; he woke up the entire block. He was not popular in my cul de sac and all of us kids hated him as well. After my grandfather died, my mother was still very fond of the rooster and wanted to keep it. No matter that we begged her and pleaded with her to get rid of it, she wouldn't do it. It was a last reminder of her father.

Complaining neighbors finally took their toll on my mother, but it took about six months. On the day of Barney's demise, my mother decided that her eight children needed some schooling on nature. She wanted to create a teaching moment. We had not had to kill and pluck chickens ever—we got our meat like God intended meat to be had—we

Lin Laurie

shopped for it and brought home body parts from the grocery store.

One Saturday afternoon she made all of us, including my stepfather, line up in the back yard. She had a table she used to position the rooster's head on. She grabbed up the rooster and pulled out a small, dull axe that had been in the garage. It took several whacks with the axe before she drew blood. As soon as the first drops were splashed into the air, I turned my back and ran into the house. My brothers stayed for the next part of the massacre while I hid in my bedroom.

After she finally was able to sever the rooster's head, it did what I'd heard—the body jumped around the backyard and she chased it around. I peeked out from my bedroom window in time for it to thud up against the window and leave a smear of blood behind. By the time the body came to rest, there was a blood bath in the backyard. My brothers all disappeared and she hosed down the backyard to remove the gory traces of "nature."

My mother plucked the feathers from the rooster and then she wrapped it in freezer paper and it went into the back of the freezer as she wasn't able to completely part with the bird. Several months later, my stepfather snuck it out and disposed of it.

That was nature at our house.

If I hadn't figured it out before, I knew now that we were a very strange family. No one else that I knew was killing roosters in their backyard. Thank God!

My Mother and a Mirror

My mother was once a model in NYC, after I was born. She was sixteen at the time and had to support a new born daughter.

In her mid-twenties, she became a Playboy bunny in Nevada, while she was trying to establish residency so she could get a quick divorce and marry my stepfather.

I've always known I looked like my mother and it has always made me very uncomfortable. People have always come up to us and asked if we were sisters. But I never felt I was beautiful and I would never have considered signing up to work wearing little more than a bathing suit and calling myself a model. I wasn't always overweight, but in my mind I was always too big, too ugly, too something. In fact, I have believed for many years that one of the reasons I struggle with my weight is because I don't feel comfortable resembling her and used food to destroy the resemblance, but it never worked.

My mother is now in her seventies. People still comment on our resemblance even though she is wrinkled from too much sun exposure and many years of smoking. On the other hand, I rarely go into the sun and have never smoked. I look like a smooth-faced red-headed ghost and I stand out in a city full of bronzed sun worshippers. I am still uncomfortable about the resemblance and even more disturbed by her wrinkles. It has kept me from seeing her as much as I would like because seeing her is like seeing my future and I hate the idea of getting old. I love my mother very much, but one thing has nothing to do with the other.

I hate to admit to the vanity of those feelings. I am vain and don't want to grow old.

Hunting for Dinner

One day, my stepfather decided to take up pheasant hunting. He bought a gun, talked his best friend into joining him, and went off into the wilderness for a weekend of hunting. What he did there was anyone's guess, but he did eventually return with four pheasants.

He tried to talk my mother into cooking them for dinner. She was skeptical. I'm not sure if my mother knew how to dress a pheasant, but she refused to try. He decided he would shelve the issue by freezing the pheasants, feathers, little bird feet, and all.

Whenever I'd get anything out of the freezer, I would steer clear of the pheasants. I'd imagined their little stiff feet, beaks pointed upward, wrapped in paper, and I'd shudder. I never wanted to touch the packages their little bodies were wrapped in. It was sort of like the game "Don't Step on a Crack or You'll Break Your Mother's Back" game. If I didn't touch them, life would go on as normal. As if!

One night, while all of us kids were away, she and my stepfather tried to cook up the pheasants. She boiled some water and dunked the birds in, and quickly pulled off the feathers. She dressed them out and then he tried to roast the meat. They chewed a couple of pieces of the tough meat and threw out the rest.

And that was hunting in our family...

Hair Brushes & Emotional Hand Grenades

I went to the same elementary school my mother had attended as a child. That's one of the "nice" things about growing up in a small town where everyone knows everybody and all their secrets.

I was the good, helpful child who normally fit in, was quiet, and didn't express my own opinions about much.

In kindergarten, whenever anyone had a birthday, they would get to pick five friends and sit at the birthday table while everyone else sat at other tables around the room. Our teacher, Mrs. Robbins, would bring in Oreo cookies for the class, and we'd sing happy birthday and spend half an hour or so honoring the birthday boy or girl.

I loved the birthday table so much that I wanted to sit at it every time there was a birthday. I was fairly popular and I got used to having a permanent seat at the table. After some months of sitting at it, I was not called up and I threw a tantrum, kicking and screaming on the floor in the room where we ate, napped, and played each day.

The principal of the school, Mrs. Jacobus, pulled me out of the class, called my mother to come down to the school, and to attend to her "willful" child. My mother hurried down—we lived only blocks from the school—carrying a plastic hair brush with pointed bristles.

Mrs. Jacobus showed her to an empty room with a table and two chairs. And there was the hair brush. My mother proceeded to beat the non-conformity right out of me. In the moment of the beating, I got one of my first tastes of feeling inferior, not belonging, and being just plain bad. Obviously that bad needed to be whipped right out of me and that's what she did.

Be a good girl, stay inside the lines of acceptable behavior, and maintain the appropriate attitude.

Those were the messages drilled into me with each slap of the brush against my skin.

Interestingly enough, when I returned to the classroom, I was given a seat at the birthday table. Each month for the rest of the year, the birthday table held an extra seat for me. I was a little confused by this message...

Dead Mother in a Corner of the Room

My stepfather married my mother when I was ten years old. He obviously loved her a lot to marry her and take care of her six kids, plus having two more sons with her. He used to delight in telling us that he loved her so much, that if she were to die, he'd want to keep her around, stuffed and naked, in a corner of dining room so she could watch over us each day as we ate. Naked. Really?

Now I know he was teasing, but at the vulnerable age of ten, this was the most horrid thing I could imagine. I'd have nightmares about my naked mother, at an age where I was just starting to mature. A stiff, cold, naked, dead mom, sitting in a corner of the room—what a vision! I knew about taxidermy so I assumed it could be done. I imagined her standing, like a cougar, cornered with her hands up high with hands shaped like claws and her teeth bared.

Lin Laurie

Over the years he stopped talking about having her naked but he always thought he'd still like to keep her around until he too was dead and then they could both be buried together. But I no longer have to fear that I would now find my seventy+ year old mother naked in the corner of their tiny house in northern California. Today, if she dies, I can take comfort in the fact that she would be wearing clothing.

Today, my mother is in bad health and one day while my stepfather and I were talking about things that might happen, he was saying that he hoped he outlasted her because she really needed to be cared for. I asked him then, what he would do when she died?

"I'm going to get me one of them Internet girlfriends," he said with a smile.

"But your mom will always be near me. I still intend to keep her in the corner," he continued on.

I laughed, but that night the images of my younger mother, naked and alone in a corner, visited me again.

By now, I have a lot of evidence that my family is totally weird. If I were still collecting evidence to support that idea, I wouldn't have to look far. But I also know that my stepdad has spent the last 45 years devoted to my mother, still in love with her as the day they first met, and I am happy my mother found someone to accept and love her; someone as weird as she is.

Stuttering

I saw the movie, The King's Speech, today. It reminded me that when I was a child, I too was a stutterer. It happened when I got to kindergarten, and lasted about two years. I had to go to speech therapy class, and eventually was cured.

As an adult, one day my mother was talking about the stuttering problem one of her children had. But she attributed it to my brother, Rick. In the instant, she invalidated my experience, and mistook my story for that of one of my brothers.

Many times since then, she has mentioned stories of things that happened to her children. In each case, she thought it was one of the brothers. Apparently, in her eyes, nothing ever happened to me. Yet I bore scars from breaking the window, scars from being hammered on by my brothers, and scars for many of the other things that occurred while I was growing up. I know these things were true and that they happened to me, even when the scars weren't visible.

My mother can't keep any of us straight, and even thought I was a girl and therefore different from the rest of the group, she still didn't see me as a distinct person and invalidated events in my life. I was unloved. I didn't matter. It took me many years to understand that two people can be in the same room, viewing the same event, and have completely different stories about what happened. That's why witnesses are seen to be weak when they testify in court as to what they've seen. And that is why my mother will never see my life through my eyes. I realize now it doesn't matter. What does matter is that she loves me, regardless of what she remembers of my life.

The Brothers

Taken en masse, I call the group of seven "the brothers." They were not referred to as my brothers as that would be too personal. They are a group, a band, a gaggle, a brood of testosterone-poisoned males, whose presence all together at once is often too much for me to contend with.

I like to take them individually—I can deal with them better that way. Let me introduce you to them in birth order:

Rick is the oldest boy. Today he is in prison for selling drugs. I am sooo proud. Not. My father adopted him and myself when we were very young and neither of us knew we weren't part of my dad's genetic offspring until I was fourteen.

Adventures with Ambien and Other Stories

Raymond is the first son by my father (who is really my adopted father). Today he is married, has three boys of his own, and is the stepfather to three daughters. He lives in Oakland with his wife and youngest son and is a crane operator.

Robert (Bob) is the second of my father's real children. He recently divorced one of my best friends, and has no children of his own. He works as a painter in Sacramento.

Earl Wayne was originally named John, for one of my uncles, but early on, my mother had a problem with that uncle and renamed my brother Earl. One day we called him John and the next day he had a whole new name. We all called him Wayne the Pain when we were growing up. He lives in Santa Cruz with his girlfriend who is either stupid or saintly for staying with him. I like her and tell her to run from him but she never listens. He suffers from addictive personality disorder, and struggles to stay employed and out of jail. He has one daughter, Sierra, who is my favorite niece and nearly my own daughter.

Russell, or Russ died at the age of forty-five about two years ago by either having a heart attack and crashing into a tree about four miles outside of the town my mom and step-father live, or crashing into a tree, bringing on a massive heart attack. It doesn't really matter—dead is dead. He was a painter and in the last few years of his life he struggled with addiction to drugs that his brother Wayne introduced him to. He has a smart, beautiful daughter named Amber, who is in Chico now, studying to become a vet.

Roy, is the first son of my stepfather and mom's marriage. He is ten years younger than I am and he is my favorite brother. He was like my child when we were growing up, and we have always remained close. He lived with me on and off as he grew up. He lives in Washington State with his wife and two sons. He is good, sweet, kind, and I love him with all my heart.

Robin, the youngest, and the second child between my mother and step-father, was a troubled child and today is a very troubled man. He was just released from prison, after serving about ten years for elder abuse. He beat up my parents badly when they asked him to move out from their house when he was about thirty-two. I don't speak to him and I am fearful he may find me when he is paroled to San Diego and I am the only family member in town. I don't want to see him but I am concerned about him. I was once a victim of his temper, as were most of my other brothers, so none of us really want to have anything to do with him.

I recently reached his parole officer and asked that a condition of parole be added where he cannot contact me. And I also found a program called Second Chance in San Diego, that will help people getting released from prison by offering a ninety day work program and will help them find a job. He was accepted and I hope he will complete the program and lead a successful life after he completes the program.

As I said, they are a gang of guys, a bundle of boys, a great big pile of maleness. In my teenaged years I mostly fed them, helped them with their homework, and did the daily parenting while my parents worked to support us.

One of my weekly duties was to go grocery shopping for what we ate Monday-Friday. I was given fifty dollars a week to feed them. Sometimes my parents would eat with us but usually they fended for themselves. We ate things like burgers, spam, hot dogs—cheap things to fill us up. I counted pennies; trying to make the most of the money I was given. If I managed to find enough items to fill us up, then I could also buy some chocolate chips and make us a batch of chocolate chip cookies. My brothers would kill for those cookies in those days.

Later in life they'd tell me that when they think of home cooking, they think of my cooking and want their wives to get my macaroni and cheese recipe. I laugh, but it is sad that this is their memory, and not a memory of us laughing and carrying on over breakfast while my mother made flap jacks or something. But it is what it is...

When I was growing up, eating was a challenge for me. If I put everything I cooked on the table and turned my back, there would be nothing left but the odor of food in the air. They were quick when it came to grabbing their food, so I learned that in order to survive I either had to eat while standing and cooking, or put something out for myself before I sat anything down on the table. That table was the black hole when it came to meal time. I'm sure I learned my bad eating habits during that time.

I love my brothers but they are very difficult for me to take as a group. I try to deal with them individually.

Family Life

When we came home from school, I would help my brothers with their homework. I didn't do mine until later in the evening after my other chores were done. Then our first job was to get our rooms cleaned. I cleaned the house and did the vacuuming and dusting, while my brothers would take everything on the floors of their bedrooms and push it under their beds. They'd make their beds

Adventures with Ambien and Other Stories

with the spreads hanging down to the floor so you couldn't tell they'd stuffed everything in there.

Usually my stepfather would perform "inspection" when he got home. This meant that he would check each room of the house to make sure it was cleared of debris and then my brothers would be able to come out and watch TV. If they didn't pass inspection we would all get into trouble. Fortunately, my stepfather wasn't very critical about the boys' rooms.

After dinner we'd all gather around my parents and sit and watch television but today I have a hard time visualizing us doing this. We'd overflow the couch and sit or lay on the floor and jostle for a good viewing position.

Punishment was something I seldom received when I was a teenager. My brothers, on the other hand, did things like sneaking out the back window and running around the neighborhood, hitting each other, and just generally doing what they shouldn't. My step-father dealt out a punishment called "on your nose."

He said that it was something he learned in the Navy, but when I tried to Google it I couldn't find any data on it. You had to lay face down on the floor. A wood floor was the best as it caused more pain than a carpet. You were supposed to balance

Lin Laurie

the weight of your head on your nose until he told you to get up. I tried it one time and if you did it correctly, it was very painful. My brothers would usually just lay there with their foreheads taking the weight of their head. Usually they would be allowed up within about thirty minutes but it could be extended for as long as sixty minutes, depending on the severity of their actions.

I can count on one hand the number of times I was punished as a teenager. On one occasion, I was caught taking my mother's car out for a drive. I had been doing that for a while and my mother remained unaware. I would wait until she fell asleep and then take the keys from her purse and sneak out and pick up my girlfriends. We'd cruise Jack in the Box for boys or drive around and feel grown up and free or some such silly nonsense. But one night, I brought it back so late that there was no dew on it when she went out to start it up. So she waited until I did it the next time, and she locked up every door and window in the house, thinking I'd have to ring the doorbell when I got home and that's how I would be busted. Oh, no, that's not what happened at all.

I crept around the house trying each door and window. Finally, I found that my own window was open but it was up too high for me to get in. I drug a picnic bench over to the window and was able to slide the window open. Then I did a Spiderman move and walked myself down the wall (I was in gymnastics at the time and was third in the county) so I was very flexible. I dropped onto the floor and closed the window as quietly as possible. I didn't know my parents were in their bedroom laughing their butts off at how far I would go to not ring the doorbell.

That act of rebellion cost me six more months of driving with my permit and some serious restriction time. They postponed letting me get my driver's license and made me drive with one of them in the car. Talk about torture.

My father surprised me that Christmas with a Honda 50 scooter. I had no idea why he did that, except maybe to thwart my mom and stepfather because in California, at fifteen and a half, you could ride a scooter or motorbike during daylight hours without having an adult present. It had never occurred to me to want a scooter, but I enjoyed the freedom and responsibility of riding one that year.

Eventually my brothers took it out dirt biking and brought it back in shreds but by that time I'd gotten my license and could drive whenever I wanted so it no longer held much interest for me.

It's funny how parents don't want you to drive UNTIL they discover how convenient it is for them. Need something from the grocery store? I'd get it.

Lin Laurie

Need to get one of my brothers to some activity? I'd be happy to oblige. It didn't take long to convince them of the wisdom of letting a sixteen year old run off with their car.

The other time when I was punished, I was sixteen and I came home drunk. I'd managed to get in the house and wave at my parents while I walked down the hall to my bedroom. I thought I was safe. But my brother, Rick came into my bedroom and asked me if I wanted something from Seven Eleven. I answered back that I didn't want anything but I'd walk with him because I lived near there. I obviously didn't know who I was talking to or where I was.

My brother Rick and I had a healthy degree of competition going on. I was the good, elder child, and he was the second born and kind of a screw-up at fifteen. So he was really excited to find me drunk out of my mind and he went running to my parents to tell on me.

My mother, seeing the ghost of teenaged pregnancy at every turn, ran into my bedroom and grabbed me by the front of my shirt. She started slapping me in the face until my stepfather pulled her off of me.

"Stop Jean! She's got contacts in."

"Are you wearing your contacts?" She stopped for a minute to peer at me.

"Yes." I don't know what made me think to say that but I had already taken out my contacts. Anyhow, it had the desired effect and she stopped hitting me.

The next morning I woke up feeling fine, got out of bed and walked down the hall to the bathroom, and was shocked to see my appearance when I looked in the mirror. My eyes were black and blue and I looked like I'd been beaten up.

My brother smirked with enjoyment when I walked out of the bathroom. "Mom said you are on restriction and can't go anywhere. No school, no nothing."

It was two days before the end of the school year and I missed the last two days. In retrospect, she was probably afraid to get into trouble if anyone saw me with my bruised face, but in those days corporal punishment isn't as taboo as it is today. I was on restriction for six months for drinking. Fortunately, I found a job that summer and ended up serving about two weeks of that sentence. My stepfather talked my mother into letting me out of the house first to go to work, and eventually into having normal freedom of movement.

A Little Parental History

My mother was in a group home from the time she was a baby until about eleven years of age. At that time, my grandmother and her husband, Steve, adopted her and brought her home to their farm. Unfortunately, Steve died before the paperwork was finalized on the adoption, so my mother was required to move back to the group home.

It took over two more years for my grandmother to find and marry another man, my grandfather Pete, and to get my mother back into her home. By now my mother was thirteen years old and was having her first taste of family life.

My father (Ray) was one of four boys and two girls who lived in an alcoholic home. He and all of his siblings were taken away from my grandmother and put into foster homes. My dad used to speak about those days as being horrible and emotionally painful. He was made to work, could not attend school, and was forced to stare down the same food daily until he ate it, starved, or it molded up.

When he was twelve, he ran away from the foster home he'd been placed at, preferring to live on the streets and by his wits. He only had a 6th grade education, but he lived in a bowling alley and stacked pins for rent. He stole from ice machines to eat, and he joined the Army at the age of sixteen, lying about his age in order to get in sooner so he could get off the streets. He became a paratrooper, jumping out of planes in the Korean War, eating rations, tromping through rice fields, and facing death at every turn. My father was incredibly proud of his time in the Army. He became a paratrooper and his favorite picture was a silk painting of him getting ready to jump out of a plain.

When he left the Army, at the age of twenty-one, he met my grandfather and they got along really well. That's how he met my mother. He loved her until the day he died, always said he'd take her back in a minute, and he happily adopted myself and my brother Rick, treating us as his own children. I wasn't aware that he had adopted me until I was fourteen. We weren't raised to be thought of as different and adoption wasn't ever talked about. I admire my father for taking on two children that weren't his own and treating us always as if we were.

These are the parents that raised us, along with my stepfather, George. I am amazed today that they kept us fed, safe, secure, loved, and let us grow up fairly normal. I didn't appreciate how much of a gift that was until much later in life, when I found out how many of my friends were abused, abandoned, or just unloved.

As a child we always tend to look for the normal and blame our parents for that which falls outside the lines. I'm afraid I beat them up a bit over the years for not being more normal or for not having a regular-sized family. Talk about super-sizing! But knowing what I know now, I think they did a wonderful job, and I want to acknowledge them for that.

Context is really important when it comes to judging our parents. Knowing what I know now makes me understand and appreciate them more than I ever did while growing up. Sometimes the grass looks greener at the neighbor's house, but it isn't. That neighbor could be getting abused, have no food to eat, or be experiencing a million other things that didn't happen to us.

Cat Killer

When I was about four years old, I did something that I will never forget. I was walking towards the back of my grandparents' farm, and I came across a little calico kitten. My mother had warned me not to pick up the kittens because I was too rough, but I ignored her. I really loved kittens. I loved their softness, the noise and the vibration of their purr, and the cuteness of them. I always was and will be a cat person.

I picked up the kitten, and I held it close in my arms, cuddling it, loving it. I killed the kitten. I felt it grow cold in my arms and I felt my first sense of despair as I cradled its limp body and I cried. I didn't know what I'd done but I knew I'd done something very bad.

My grandfather came upon me crying, and began to yell at me for killing the kitten. I don't recall what he said, but I remember it wasn't good. He marched me up to where my mother was shelling peas, and my mother took over yelling at me.

There is a belief in some forms of therapy, that there are three moments in our lives that determine how we act in the world as adults. These moments are the genesis of self or the ID. In these moments, we make decisions about ourselves that later determine the type of mates we attract, the kind of jobs we get, and how we act. The act occurs, we form opinions and meanings about the act, and we make a decision to behave a particular way based on our opinion of that moment. This event was one of those three pivotal moments for me. I made the accidental death of my kitten mean that I was wrong, I was bad, and I was undeserving of love. It has had a monumental effect on my life.

Boys and Men

When I was in the third grade, my mom and stepdad decided to leave our small, New Jersey town, because the fact that they loved each other and wanted to be together was the town scandal. Both of them were married to other people, and they were not only carrying on a red hot love affair, but wanted to leave their spouses for each other.

Lin Laurie

At the same time, I had my first boyfriend, Tommy. Tommy was cute, smart, and dedicated to me. He carried my books home and walked me home from school. I was very puzzled by his behavior but I liked it. When I asked him why he wanted to carry my books, he said his older brother told him that's what boys do with girls. He didn't even have hormones to blame; he was just reacting to the teachings of an older male.

He tried to hold my hand and to kiss me. Again, I found these things a little puzzling, but I pretty much went along, except for the kissing thing. I wasn't into that.

Tommy said he'd love me forever.

We moved to Sparta, New Jersey for about three months, and I had to leave school. After ninety days, for some reason, we moved back to the same town and I returned to the same school.

Tommy was now telling Annette he loved her forever. I was apparently chopped liver and forever was less than ninety days. I thought of warning Annette, but decided she'd have to find out for herself how boys lied.

Here I was being left by a male and it was only the third grade! Men were dogs; I would never get married, and should therefore never show anyone that I might want to fall in love and get married.

After all, that's what happened when you're unlovable—people leave you.

This was another one of those pivotal moments where something happened and then I made it mean something more, something negative, and then let it have a lasting effect on my life. Tommy was just a kid practicing his "moves" for later years and unfortunately I was one of his early victims.

The Uninvited One

It's funny how certain things are buried inside you but they take a major event to ever float to the surface.

I have a memory of a popular girl at school inviting most of our class to a birthday party. I was one of few people who did not receive an invitation. However, when her mother found out I hadn't been invited, she told my mother to bring me over to the house and that it must have been a mistake.

My mom and I went shopping and we bought a nice present for the girl. On the day, we went over to the girl's house and knocked on the door. When the girl opened it, she saw me and started to scream at me about how she didn't invite me and I shouldn't be there. Her mother tried to calm her down and we ended up handing over the present we'd bought and leaving the party without actually having entered the house.

Lin Laurie

It was embarrassing, uncomfortable, and memorable. I felt horrible and ashamed because someone didn't like me and didn't want me at their party. I have no idea what I did, but it didn't matter because that's how she felt about me. And of course she had the right to have whomever she wanted at her house.

Until recently, I would never go to someone's house unless I received an invitation directly from the homeowner. I do not trust casual invitations from anyone. I do not trust.

This seems like a fairly benign issue, but recently a friend of mine invited me to become part of a fitness education group where the teacher of the group was someone I knew and he'd said it was OK to invite me. Well, I wanted to call him up and verify that he did want me there and I did, but doing that offended the friend who invited me. She felt I didn't trust her when in my head it wasn't about her at all. It was about how being treated by someone when you're a child can impact the way you behave as a woman.

Lack of Understanding

The idea of people not being liked is something that we've all had to deal with. Most people seem to have some idea of what they've done and whether or not it is something they want to right or not.

On the other hand, the same lack of understanding that I had about why that girl didn't invite me to her party is something that has continued to plague me throughout the years. I attract people to me and don't understand why they act the way they do. This problem hasn't occurred every day, but occasionally I seem to make people crazy.

I worked on contract for a company in Washington State in 2002-2003. From the day I first walked in the door, there was a man who worked there that I'll call Gus. He seemed to have a heightened sense of awareness of me and was attentive to anything I did. We were in a really large cubicle and whenever I would get up to walk to the bathroom or to take a break, he would turn around in his chair and watch me.

No one else seemed to notice his behavior, but it was very disturbing to me. Eventually I asked to move to the other side of the cubicle where I was closer to him, but couldn't see him due to a wall that separated us. This helped but he started trying to walk me out to my car several times and sat next to me when we went out to eat as a group. I was very uncomfortable but I didn't know what to do. I didn't encourage him but I wasn't rude either. To this day I'm not sure if there was something else I could have done or if he was just a weirdo.

Lin Laurie

Gus was a very odd man in general, and used to talk throughout the day about how people hated him at another company he worked at and they threw lab experiments at him (he worked in a laboratory), or about how he drank every night. Not to mention that he was a gun nut and would talk about shooting things in his house. Oh, he was an attractive guy—yeah. What a catch!

One day, when he was doing something annoying and there was no one else in the cubicle, I tried to talk to him during our lunch break.

"Look Gus, I am not interested in you so please stop."

"Why not?" He genuinely seemed puzzled.

"I am seeing someone." I made it up. I had just met someone I would end up dating, but I didn't know I'd be dating him when this event occurred.

"No you aren't." He pouted.

"Gus, you really would not like me if you knew me. I am not your type."

"Yes you are. Why won't you just go out with me—just once?" He petulantly asked as he played with his food. "What's wrong with me?"

"I'm not interested in you." I knew better than to start listing all the ways in which he was wrong with me.

He threw his onion rings at me, fortunately missing me, but he didn't actively bother me after that, thinking he could just wait out my contract, and I was lulled into thinking things were fine and he had forgotten all about me. Silly, optimistic woman that I am, I hoped things would blow over; and I thought they had. That is until he found out I was going to take a permanent job with the company and that I would be taking over web site maintenance—a job that belonged to him but that he was always too busy to do. He was very unhappy about that, and immediately started to become an obstacle to the things I needed to get from him.

Soon after that, when he was talking out loud about some of the crazy thoughts he had and he happened to say something really stupid about how people in California who were in foster care as children received extra consideration in applying for jobs. I cannot tell you why I didn't ignore him, and so I said:

"My father was in foster care growing up and that did not give him a leg up on other job applicants." I wasn't thinking that irrational people will have irrational reactions to things they don't want to hear.

Lin Laurie

I didn't say anything more at the time, and there were two other people (including a vice president) who heard me say it, so they backed me up later.

I finished the day without noticing that Gus was very quiet. I left work and I headed home. About 7 pm that night I got a call from a vice president.

"Don't come in tomorrow until 9 am and then you'll have to meet with Scott."

"OK. What's going on?" I was very puzzled as Scott and I never had a need to talk.

"Gus has complained that you have created a hostile work environment and we need to investigate."

"What? What's going on?" I was extremely puzzled. I didn't even know what "hostile work environment" meant. Being a contractor most of my life, I wasn't knowledgeable about some of the employment laws on the books.

The witnesses supported what I said but I would not go back to work while he was at the company. The company valued both of us and didn't want to get rid of either one of us but they acknowledged that he was troubled. I couldn't see how I could go back and work in close proximity to him—I didn't know what else he was capable of doing and I was pretty stunned at the entire series of events—so I chose to meet with my manager at Starbucks to exchange work while the company decided what to do. In the end, the company ordered me to return and I declined, since I wasn't yet a full-time employee, and I never did become a permanent employee.

While all this was going on, this man would call me up and say horrible things to me. I started to worry for my safety since I knew he was a gun nut and since he was also under pressure while the company investigated his complaint, I feared he might go postal. The phone calls did not help me feel better.

One night, he happened to call my house while I was having dinner with one of the heads of the Washington State Crime Lab and a Seattle police officer that I was dating at the time. I put the call on speaker phone and let my guests listen to his ranting for a while, until they motioned me to hang up. The next day I went to the police department to complain about the calls. The calls stopped for a while after he was contacted by the police. In the meantime I was getting ready to move to San Diego, thinking this was a really good time in my life to create some changes and that maybe life would be better somewhere else where he wasn't.

Gus was sentenced to probation for the phone calls and I didn't think any more about it for a few months. That's not true; actually I was so angry

Lin Laurie

about it that it took me a few months to come down off the ceiling about the entire series of events.

I moved to California, worked on therapy by writing a letter I would never send where instead of being angry about everything that happened, I started out with an ugly letter that stated everything he did that was awful. Then I took everything he did and looked at the results of his actions as a new opportunity. It worked wonderfully, and I calmed down and went to work at a new company, thus beginning my new California life.

Apparently Gus could not stop thinking of me, and soon I started to receive the most horrible emails I've ever seen (real or fiction) in my life. These emails threatened me with disgusting violence. Of course I contacted Seattle Police and he subsequently was convicted of violating a restraining order and he went to prison for a year.

This is an awful story; one I seldom think about. But when I do, I wonder what I could have done different. I obviously attracted a nut (he wasn't the first nut and unfortunately, he likely won't be the last). So I still don't understand how people think or why what I did created this horrible experience. I do know that ultimately it wasn't my fault and I can't control the actions of nuts but that doesn't help me feel better. I keep thinking if only I'd done...

Internal Bleeding

When I was ten years old, I was jump roping with my friends out on the school playground. A friend at each end of the rope was twirling it, and I was jumping in and out. As I went to jump out one time, I jumped immediately into a pole and hit my head hard. I started to cry and I walked away from our game and into the bathroom.

Not to be indelicate, but I saw blood in my urine. I started screaming and crying, and the principal came into the bathroom to see what was going on.

I thought I was dying and I had brain damage. The blood was internal damages, of course. What else would a ten year old think?

The principal called my mother to come to the school to get me. She wouldn't say anything about what was wrong with me, but she gave me wet paper towels (that was for the brain damage, I thought).

I learned about periods that day. My mother was shocked that I started so young and she hadn't prepared me for anything like what happened. Of course I thought for a short time that in order to get your period you must get a head injury, but I eventually got that figured out.

Lin Laurie

In those days, menstrual pads came in one size—gigantic. Wearing one was like riding a horse when you're ten years old. I was a fairly small girl at that age. People knew. More importantly, boys knew. And boys talked about it, teased me about it, and yet had a sense of fascination about it, and made me keenly aware that it somehow set me apart.

For many years I felt like everything I did, breasts, bras, periods, and other stages of teenaged life were visible to everyone and it was one of the reasons I was so uncomfortable with my body. I was one of the girls who did everything before the rest of the girls and got the brunt of jokes and poking. I guess it made me stronger but it also made me embarrassed and self-conscious, and was one of the reasons I gained weight—to hide my body from the boys and later men.

Paralysis

When I was about seven or eight, my brother Rick and I were given a chemistry set to share. The appropriate age group for chemistry set was twelve to fifteen. It was definitely way too advanced for the two of us and I have no idea why our parents bought it for us.

I can remember putting a lot of chemicals into bottles and when mixed together they would provide some kind of visual reaction to each other.

Adventures with Ambien and Other Stories

That was pretty cool. We created smoke, changed the colors of various solutions, and we had the ability to use a very sharp set of tweezers to put small objects on slides and look at them using a pretty sophisticated microscope.

My brother and I used to fight over everything in the chemistry set. One day we were both tussling over the tweezers and he got mad and stabbed my right leg right above my knee cap. It immediately hurt like hell. My parents thought the pain would go away and eventually it did, but it temporarily paralyzed my right leg. I could not walk at all.

We consulted a doctor and he looked at x-rays of my leg but the doctor couldn't find anything wrong with me and told my parents to just take me home and wait it out.

The paralysis lasted about a week, scaring the daylights out of my parents. They weren't sure if I would ever walk again. I remember mostly being in a daze and trying not to think about whether or not I would walk.

During the week, I remember my father picking me up and carrying me places. He'd sit me down somewhere high up so I would have an unobstructed view of the other children playing. I couldn't join in and some of the kids took the opportunity to make fun of me. Sitting alone, I felt incredibly lonely, like looking through a Macy's store window at all the toys but not being able to reach any of them. The paralysis didn't last long, but that alienated view of life has stayed with me. Up until this last year, I never felt like I was truly part of something—a community, a group, anything. The world felt like them against me. It was not a great feeling.

Walking through life without a sense of truly belonging is a very difficult way to live. The distance between me and others was a huge chasm to me. I didn't realize until a few years ago that most people feel like that to some degree or another. Instead of being an alien on a strange planet, I found that just in having those feelings I really was part of a community; the community of man; the human race.

I started to realize that I have set up my life to perpetuate that feeling. Most of my life I have made a living as a contractor, insuring that all my jobs would end and I would never have that sense of belonging to a company.

My personal life was set up in a similar manner. I never admitted to wanting to be in a relationship and dated men for about six months and then would leave or somehow cause the relationship to end. I am glad to say that the feeling is receding and I am changing all aspects of my life so I don't continue on with supporting those feelings when they do not serve me at all and never did.

I recently took a class in which I stated that I wanted to be a "man magnet" to find the right man for myself. If you can't even say it, how can you find someone to love?

Learning to Fight

The school year was about to start when my family went school clothes shopping. I recall being around twelve at the time. We went to JC Penny's and the five or so of us who were in school selected the outfits we wanted, new underwear, socks, and so on. I can recall we got all the way up to the register and we may have started to ring up the clothes when my stepfather told my mother that he left his check book at home. My mother was so pissed you would think her face would explode. It was a lot of work to get that many children to pick out clothing and she didn't want to have to repeat the experience.

We drove home in deafening silence. We got out of the car and went into the house, and I remember thinking we would go back and get the clothing later after we picked up the checkbook.

Several days earlier, my stepfather had purchased a brand new stereo that coincidently cost about as much as our school clothing. My mother walked into the house and directly to the stereo equipment. She started hauling pieces out on the front lawn. We weren't paying attention at first, but the yelling my mother was doing drew us back to the front. She picked up a sledge hammer and started to slam it down into the stereo equipment as we watched. Bits of plastic and wood were flying. The speakers split apart into about four pieces each.

My stepfather was fairly quiet during this display. But once he saw what my mother was doing he started throwing things at her. It was a horrible fight, I never forgot it, and that's how I learned to handle my anger when I grew up.

I recall living with a man named Bill, and I had been commuting two hours each day to work so I was dead tired. I had just gotten home and I was heating some beef stew in a pan when he started to complain about something. I took the pan off the stove (it wasn't hot yet) and dumped the pan over his head. I saw the potatoes run over his nose, and fall off his to the ground below. Then I ran! And he chased me. Fortunately I locked myself away until he calmed down and I realized that day that I did not know how to fight with someone like an adult. I didn't want to throw food at someone so I tried to figure out a different way to fight.

When I got married, my husband was a loud, yelling type, plus he was physically imposing. He liked to rant about whatever he was mad about but that kind of display of anger just freaked me out. So I would make up lists of things I was upset about and I'd hand him the list and want to talk about it once he calmed down. I wanted a calm, rational discussion with concessions and promises. I think he wanted drama and more of a physical release for his anger. Surprise! Our marriage didn't last. What a shock!

Today I almost never fight with anyone and if I do, it is much more calm and rational than my parents fought when they were my age. My last few relationships were pretty quiet and harmonious for the most part. My parents are still married and they never fight any more. But we all learned that throwing things, destroying property, and yelling harsh words at each other doesn't work.

So why is it that there are so many people throwing cell phones when they get mad at each other today? Judge Judy, The People's Court, Judge Mathis, these are just a few of the many shows that have an abundance of cases where one party is being sued for breaking the other party's cell phone. These cases are usually the period at the end of a couple's relationship.

I guess I couldn't afford to be in a relationship today as my last cell phone cost over $400 and the iPhone I have today cost several hundred as well. But there is a lot less drama involved to sit down and discuss something; it is anticlimactic actually.

I suppose when you madly love someone you want to feel that kick of adrenalin that kicks in when you are angry. Maybe it is the absence of that which can feel boring if you are used to the mad, crazy fighting that people want because it is better than feeling nothing at all. I'm not sure but I am not giving up my cell phone to find out. I will be available to write up a list of problems anytime and anyplace.

I Have Seen Magic

If you aren't a kid from the east coast, then you probably don't know what it was like in the 50's and early 60's to view the windows at the Macy's on 34th Street in NYC. Macy's usually had the best window, full of wondrous, magical technology, toys, and other goods. Gimbels, Saks, and many of the other large department stores would make a serious effort to amaze and dazzle the hordes of people who came to view their displays. Even today, some of the larger stores continue the tradition of giving a free show to all viewers. It isn't the same now because television has jaded our view of the amazing but it is still a great show.

Each year, the newspaper would publish a list of the equivalent of the TV guide for store displays and my family would make plans to trek to NYC.

Adventures with Ambien and Other Stories

My mother would stuff us into our snowsuits. This process took some time as there were six children at the time. If you can remember the scene in Christmas Story where Ralph's brother Randy is bundled up into a snowsuit where he couldn't put his arms down, we looked like that only times six. We would walk around looking like small penguins, waddling around and flapping our arms. We took the train into New York, ending up in Grand Central Station. We'd walk along its marbled corridors out to the street, and travel en mass, following the map my father had made.

The first store was always like viewing a miracle in process. Whatever the display, it took your breath away, and providing a benchmark of whatever would come after. We would gather at a window, impatiently wait our turn to get close to the window as we couldn't see anything until the crowd in front of us cleared away. Then, we'd feast our eyes on the spectacular display, and eventually, way too soon, we'd be pushed and pulled out from the front of the story so another group of people could have a few magical moments with the windows.

Magic surely described the animation and miniature sets that in some cases took all year to produce. To us kids, this night was like having a peak at Santa's workshop, exciting our imagination, and giving us visuals for our dreams for many nights to come.

Lin Laurie

This was a once-a-year experience that was the equivalent of seeing back stage at a Broadway show, like peeking at the machinations that go on behind the scenes. I can recall looking forward to that night even more than Christmas day. It was an east coast event that meant something incredible when I was a kid. It continues today, but the competition to be the best window is waning along with budgets and the erosion of the brick and mortar department stores. It doesn't generate the same sense of awe and wonder as it used to have when I was growing up but it is still a great event if you happen to visit NYC around Christmas. It was an isolated moment of togetherness for a loud, messy family.

Boys and Men Revisited

When I was seventeen, I had a friend named Eric. He was like a puppy dog that followed me around. He and two of his friends (John and Ray) hung with me and my friends Linda and Susan.

I wasn't interested in Eric at first. He was nice, he had a little acne, drove his own car at seventeen, had a job, and he really liked me. We hung around a lot and eventually we started to date. It seemed like I was just starting to get attached to him when John and Ray decided to take a motorcycle out one day and they ran into a wall, causing Ray to be killed, and John was severely brain-damaged.

Adventures with Ambien and Other Stories

Around this time, my parents decided we needed to move away to a simpler place (I lived in the SF bay area in the sixties when hippies were moving to Haight Ashbury in droves). Eric was absolutely devastated at the loss of his friends and that was compounded by my leaving. About a month after I moved away, he committed suicide by overdosing on drugs.

What was worse, everyone thought I couldn't take hearing about it and they tried to protect me. I wasn't able to attend the funeral because I didn't know about his death until after the funeral had been held. It never occurred to me until today that he may have done it partially because I moved away, on top of having one friend die and another essentially die as well. As far as I know, there was no note, so I don't know.

I really resented the idea that I was unable to take hard news. My brothers did the same thing to me when my father had a heart attack and needed a double bypass. No one called me, and I lived in Seattle by then, until after he'd had bypass surgery.

When I heard that they had kept the news of my father's illness from me, I was incredibly angry. Not only was I cheated out of a moment to morn a boyfriend as a teenager, but I was almost cheated out of the opportunity to say goodbye to my father, as an adult.

Lin Laurie

Fortunately he didn't die then, and later in life when he was sick, they didn't do the same thing again, so I had an opportunity to participate fully in my father's life for the last couple of months of his life and I also had the opportunity to say goodbye to him. My other brothers didn't get that same opportunity, but at least it was at their own choice and not because they were protected from knowing the truth.

The fact that I did get to say goodbye has given me a great deal of peace over the last eight years since his death. And I wouldn't have had that time to talk with my father if my family had again kept his illness from me.

In my family, everyone (the brothers) thinks I am somehow the weak one because I easily cry and they are men who don't want to hurt their sister. They think that I hurt more because I show tears and they don't want to hurt me. But I am absolutely clear that in NOT telling me what is going on, they actually cause me more upset because they keep me from being able to react to the moment. I know they mean well, but you don't do anyone a service by protecting them. Protecting them is only easier for you as it helps you avoid dealing with people's feelings. You only throw up walls. They all know now not to spare me but fortunately I haven't had to deal with a lot of personal loss up until this point.

For years I believed that not only was I unlovable, but that I needed to appear strong and invulnerable to people or they would keep things from me. It didn't help me in learning to trust in this world.

Life is a Carnival Old Friend

I worked in a carnival for two weeks one summer as a teenager; I was fifteen. I worked the coin toss where they place flat, glass plates on top of very large stuffed animals. I should tell you now that these games are rigged against you. No, they don't grease the plates, although a lot of people believe that to be the trick. But they use only glass plates, which have a higher slide ability, and they place the plates at a particular level to make it difficult to win. People do still win so it is possible to do it. The odds are just not in favor of your winning anything.

My job was to encourage the jocks, jokers, and the local yokels to have a toss and win a big furry toy for a wife or girlfriend. It was easy for a long haired teenager to flick her hair and get the attention of the boys and men and that was the audience who was attracted to these games. This is where I first learned I might actually be attractive.

The manager of these games, Luke, said he was in love with me. He was cute, 24, and very persuasive. He wanted me to run off with him where we would live happily ever after continually moving from town to town with the carnival. I didn't think so. I didn't see myself living that kind of life. I enjoyed what I was doing because it broke up the boredom of summer and gave me some male attention, but I did not succumb to his charms, worked out my two weeks, and left the carnival, to the relief of my mother.

I remember being puzzled at how someone could know me for a couple of weeks and say they loved me. It was another instance where the behavior of the opposite sex was really puzzling to me and I didn't buy into it at all. I thought he was crazy and was glad when the carnival moved on.

I realized later that my mother thought, feared, imagined, that I would find something more enticing that high school in Fremont, California, and that I would run off and get pregnant with eight children. When she found out that I was working at the carnival, she had a fit. But I was also getting old enough to fight back and I kept my job for the two weeks they were in town.

With knowledge, comes power. Once I knew that what drove her to restrict my behavior was routed in fear that I'd get pregnant and end up powerless like she felt, I knew how to drive her absolutely crazy. I also made up my mind at that point that I didn't want to have any children and I wanted to have control over my own life. That fall, I withdrew from public high school and started taking college classes. I quickly graduated from hanging around with teenage boys to dating college men. Talk about a blow for independence!

Talk about making my mother nuts!

My mother once told me once that she envied my life, where I could write, work wherever I wanted, and was basically free. The funny thing is that while I never missed having children, I did miss having that sense of security that a family brings to the table. I have never felt acceptance, love, and the ability to take relationships for granted that she got from creating her own family.

High School Blues

When I was in high school, I wouldn't exactly say I was a geek, but I was in every music class my school offered (five), got A's in science classes, and overall had a pretty easy time learning the material. I hung out with a group of girls who were like me, not the prettiest or the most popular, but fiercely loyal to each other. I wasn't part of a "click" and there weren't really any boys who hung out with us. We were "good" girls who didn't drink, weren't interested in drugs (this was the 70's) and we adhered to the expectation s of our parents. Even then, I could see the start of what turned out to be some serious compartmentalization issues.

Lin Laurie

When school was over, I'd completed my hours of band practice, done all my chores, and fulfilled any other obligations I turned into a completely different person and I hung out with two girls from another school. Linda and Sue were way more on the edge of life than I was. Linda was my best friend and the one who taught me to hitchhike, sneak out of the house at night, and to try pot with first the first time. I loved my "bad girl" friends. In retrospect, we weren't all that bad, but at the time it seemed like we were wild, carefree rebels.

It is ironic that a few years after I met Linda, I ended up running away from home. When her mother learned that I'd done that, I became the "bad" girl of the group. She assumed I was the one her taught her daughter to party and to like boys. If she only knew that all her kids had reputations as being the partiers. I just didn't want to be at home with my family and it scared her because she didn't want her daughter to follow in my footsteps. I can't say I blame her but at the time I was very upset at not being able to easily see my best friend.

With my "good girl" friends I dated the high school quarterback for a summer, tried out for letter girls, played flute in all my bands, and even started to pick up the piccolo. Eventually I became the piccolo player for our marching band, and any mistakes you make being the sole piccolo player were very noticeable; I got pretty good at that point and I really enjoyed playing any kind of music with others.

I started a life-long love affair with computers in the summer before my sophomore year. I talked my way into a business class a year before I was supposed to be eligible and I learned first how to keypunch, and next how to use a variety of other business equipment. Once I conquered the simpler machines, my teacher started to show me how to program.

The first language I learned was Cobol. I had to punch up a deck of cards containing my program and then submit it to someone who would run it on the school machines at night and then give me a printout of the results the next day. It was very hands off, but the relationship I developed with my teacher and learning I received around programming computers would come back when I was twenty to help me learn another language (RPG), which I used and made a very nice living creating custom financial applications with for the following ten years.

Mr. Delahoy, who died a few years ago, volunteered to teach me RPG after his regular classes were over and until I could get into a junior college programming class. My boss at the time let me off work early so I could drive up to Fremont from San Jose to make the private weekly class, also let me use his computer during off hours to run my programs. He also encouraged me to read the ten or so computer operations books for the IBM equipment we had at the time whenever I was done with my regular work. That was one of the most boring tasks I've ever taken on but it proved to be very helpful. Both men gave me valuable gifts of their support and in doing that, probably significantly changed the direction of my career.

Neither of my groups mingled with each other. If I was "bad" I did it away from school. If I acted nerdy, I did it with my school friends. I didn't understand until many years later that this separation behavior was a way for me to compartmentalize various aspects of myself and to this day I work at merging the pieces of myself into one cohesive person who has experienced many different ways of being but isn't defined by any single one of them.

Popular Girls

In junior high and the first year of high school my biggest wish was to be one of the "in" girls. They dressed better, had the current hair styles, had the attention of all the boys, and just seemed to have an easier time with school life. They were the cool ones and they only talked to their own kind.

Many years later, I ran into the girl I considered the most popular of everyone in "the" click and having the perspective of about ten years of adult experience, I asked her what it was like being in that group. I don't recall exactly how I worded the question, but that was the gist of it. I can't recall her name now, but I think it was Karen. We ran into each other at a Starbucks and sat down to have coffee together after recognizing me. I had no idea what to say to her but I have always been a curious, question-asking, fool, so whenever I had nothing to say, I let my natural curiosity take over. Her answer really surprised me.

"I was scared all the time." She sipped her coffee.

"What were you scared of? I thought your life would be easy since you were so accepted." I was very intrigued.

"I remember you and how I always thought yours was the better life because your friends accepted you. I was afraid every day that something would happen to make them stop liking me and I'd be cast out of the group and have no friends. It was awful." Karen twirled her straw as she spoke.

I'd never considered myself to be fortunate not to be popular before. I'd come to realize somewhere in high school that popularity wasn't the end of the universe but I'd never considered what life would be like from her perspective.

Lin Laurie

That short conversation really made a difference in my life. After that day, I was very conscious of my actions any time I started envying anyone else's life. Besides being a waste of time and energy, I realized that things looked different when you were on the outside of someone's life, relationship, job, etc., and you have no way of knowing what it is like inside. And you probably don't even have the tools to imagine it.

I try to be careful of what I wish for and that is the moral for me. I also try to love ad value loyal friends, not those who seem to be more fun, more educated, or more cool. My friends have never kicked me out of the crowd because I have a selfish, uncool, or unpopular moment. My friends have substance and they give me love, trust, and loyalty so that I become substantial as well. How cool is that?

Best Friends and Brain Surgeons

One of my first best friends in New Jersey was named Susan and she became a brain surgeon. She is one of the many Susan's I've befriended over the years. I don't know why, but I seem to attract people with that name... Anyhow, she was twelve and I was ten when we first met in West Caldwell, New Jersey. If the town sounds familiar to you, it may be because North West Caldwell was the fictional home of Tony Soprano. She lived in the ritzy development that was part of a tract of ritzy homes that divided the back end of my street with a high, wooden fence. We first met because she was trying to catch frogs in the brook that ran behind her house and into my part of the hood.

The brook, aptly named "Big Brook," by myself at about 8 years of age, was part of a dividing line between the "haves" and the "have not's." Susan's father was some kind of attorney who worked in New York City. They lived in this big, beautiful home where everything had a place. It was a calm, orderly oasis to me and I always wanted to play at her house.

On the other hand, I lived in a large, messy house, where there was never a place for anything, toys and brothers were scattered everywhere, and I really hated living there then. Actually, I've always hated it. I live a well-ordered existence today that probably had a lot to do with my experiences back then.

It's funny how we expect something to look and to be a certain way and when it doesn't look that way in life, we invalidate it. It took me most of my life to get over the fact that I came from a big, boisterous, chaotic, loving family because it didn't look like Beaver Cleaver's family. It's only now that I can say, yeah, I do come from a big, loud, crazy family and I

Lin Laurie

have a lot of big, untidy brothers who love me. How awesome is that?

Susan was Jewish and didn't attend regular school. I think that had a lot to do with why we were friends even though there was more than a two year difference in our ages. She was exotic in her differences and she was incredibly smart. I was totally envious of her life.

Susan told me once that she envied my life because she thought that all that messy jumble of brothers and the rest of life meant that we all loved each other more and she felt a lack of love in her family.

I could write for days on the joyful times I spent at her house or out catching frogs or lightening bugs. I loved her, she was my first best friend, and other than one fight we had (over whose frogs were whose), and we always got along.

I've only seen her once as an adult, when I went to NYC for a visit and we spent the day together. We went to the Metropolitan Museum of Art and saw a Monet exhibit.

One thing she mentioned that day was that how different her life had been from mine on the inside. Her father had been a gambler and sometimes things were so tight that their electricity would be cut off or there wouldn't be enough food to eat. The entire family was driven by the ups and downs in fortune that the father suffered and they never knew what was going to happen daily. Would they eat hamburgers or filet mignon? Would there be heat and lights? From my perspective, they had a beautiful house, an exotic and well-ordered life on the greener side of the grass. I'd had no idea what the reality was.

When we were kids, we used to love playing with our troll dolls. We had all sizes and colors with matching outfits and accessories. When I came to visit her, Susan took me back to her house that day and I got to meet her husband. I also got to find out that when she'd moved out of her parent's house many years ago, one of the items she felt compelled to keep was her box of troll dolls. I was so touched that she would keep them and that they meant that much to her.

We stayed in touch for probably 25 years or so. I grew up to become a software developer at that point and later a technical writer. Susan became a brain surgeon. I always knew she'd been smart. But the first time she told me what she did, I had to smile, thinking about the girl whom I'd played trolls with, dressed up our cats with, and even ordered my first Chinese meal with could turn out to be a person who would surgically operate on people's brains. Wow. That still blows me away.

Lin Laurie

We lost touch somewhere along the way. I think it was because of something I did and I have always felt bad and guilty without knowing exactly what I did. But I am so sorry because she is someone I would love to have back in my life. She is a person with major substance and I will always love her.

One Different Thing

When I think about my life and the way it has turned out so far, there is one single thing that I know, had I made a different decision, would have completely changed my life.

I never slept with the high school quarterback.

If I had, here is what would have happened: I would have gotten pregnant, I would have gotten married, and I would have ended up in Bend Oregon with several children and a gorgeous looking cabinet maker who is totally computer illiterate. And I am absolutely sure that I would have been miserable.

I know this is what would have happened because that's exactly what happened to the girl he dated after I moved away. She got pregnant and they got married. The marriage lasted about twenty years and they had two or three children. I know that could have been my life and I am so glad that it wasn't. I loved his family and knew them really well since they lived across the street from my family for many years.

Adventures with Ambien and Other Stories

When I was in the sixth grade, we moved to Fremont and I had to start going to a new school. The first day, I remember walking into the gym with the principal to view the entire class holding hands and dancing in a circle. This was California in the sixties and they were learning to dance. I remember this huge sense of fear and intimidation and wondering how I would ever breach the group or fit in. But John, all six feet of him, broke free of the hand he was holding and held his hand out to me. I can still see his hand, reaching out for mine. I still remember the feeling of holding his big, safe hand, and I think I fell for him that day.

We'd had a flirtation on and off for years after that but it wasn't until we were both sixteen that we dated each other. I had no idea until much later in life that many of the girls at my high school were jealous of me because I knew him really well and lived across the street from him. It was another case of having no idea what other people thought about me.

We had just started to seriously date when summer came between our sophomore and junior years. He committed to bike to Oregon that summer and would be gone over a month. While he was away, my parents broke the news to us that we'd be moving away—to Bend, Oregon. How ironic that he'd end up there years later.

Lin Laurie

During the year before my 30th high school reunion, I located him through one of his sons (thank goodness for computers) and we had a really wonderful phone conversation. I lived in Seattle at the time but was getting ready to move to San Diego. I was trying to decide whether to go to the reunion and I realized that the only person I was really curious to see was him so I picked up the phone and called.

Minor in the Class

I started at Ohlone College in Fremont, California the fall of what would have been my junior year in high school. I was sixteen. I'd gotten tired of the silly things they taught you in high school and I arranged to get my GED and leave high school far behind. I was not being challenged as a student.

This would have been in 1972, and college was a heady place to be for a teenager. I rode my ten-speed to school, sat on the grass with the older kids, listened to them talk about lots of interesting things that weren't discussed in high school. The boys (actually they were young men) had long hair and looked sexy and sophisticated. I was sixteen, cute, and made new friends easily. I didn't hurt for dates either.

Being so young, I stood out and made a lot of new friends. It was heady stuff to be talking with people a few years older than I was and who listened to my thoughts. I loved college and to this day school is a wonderful place for me to be. I love the learning, the exchange of ideas, and the ability to meet new people interested in the same things I was interested in. I still love the challenge of learning new things and whether I teach or attend, I love education. I don't understand why everyone doesn't want to go to school.

Bridge Issues

In the summer of 2001 I decided to bring my seven year old niece with me on a trip from Seattle to California. I had just closed my technical writing business I'd had for over five years and I wanted to get away before I started working again for an actual boss. I was driving my two-year old Taurus, a comfortable, mid-sized car with a V6 engine. We made it from Seattle to Yreka the first day and I found a hotel room for us to spend the night. We swam, ate dinner, and watched movies in our room. I slept well, and we got on the road early, after a quick breakfast.

I was fine until we started coming down the mountain around Lake Shasta. I noticed I was feeling a little nauseous as the road twisted and turned and I started to favor the middle or left-most lane. I had recently been suffering a little stomach upset so I thought little of it.

Lin Laurie

I went from highway 5 to the 505 before Sacramento. The 505 is a nice, straight road and an easy, boring ride, so there was no problem there. Then I transitioned to the 80 and drove to Vallejo. The Carquinez Strait cuts between Solano and Contra Costa Counties. The bridge across the Strait is called the Benicia-Martinez Bridge; it's a metal bridge with steel grating that you can see through-- all the way down into the water. I know because I looked—this turned out to be a big mistake.

Next came the 580 west over the Richmond-San Rafael bridge. This was like a roller coaster ride and by now I was driving about 45 miles an hour and couldn't go any faster. My hands were sweating like crazy and every word out of my mouth was Oh F... I was crying and my niece was also scared. She'd never seen me act like this before. I was grateful to a semi-truck driver who followed very close behind me—close, but not tailgating, and he protected me from the anger of other drivers as we inched at a snail's pace across the bridge.

By now I was terrified, panic-stricken, and even though I knew it was all in my head, it didn't matter. I survived the crossing of the 580 and started south on Highway 1. From that point out I only drove over small bridges between hills. Every one of them was a huge obstacle and I didn't know what I would do when I got to the Golden Gate Bridge. I did know that there was no way in hell I'd be able to cross it in my current state. My stomach was feeling sicker and sicker with each mile I drove.

We stayed in Mill Valley overnight and had dinner with some friends who tried to help me figure out what to do. The next morning one of them drove me across the Golden Gate Bridge while I sat in the back seat with my head in a pillow. Another friend followed behind us. When we got to San Francisco, my friend went back in the other car and I headed down to San Jose to see some of my family. I was completely freaked out by this time.

My brother Wayne, who is my niece's father, ended up driving me back to Seattle and then I paid to fly him back to San Jose. The good side of this was that he hadn't spent much time with my niece and so he got to spend a week with her and he thanks me to this day for the opportunity to get to know her better. I slept all the way home and tried not to look out the window of the car because by the time we went back, every road edge of the road caused me to feel real fear.

When I got back to Seattle, I did a little research and found that bridge phobia is a common anxiety disorder, that it occurs most often in women and it has a name: Gephyrophobia. One cause is lack of control, which made sense to me because I had just closed down a business I'd had for the last five years and was about to start a new job. I definitely had control issues. The road to recovery was desensitization—I had to face my fears and bridges until the terror went away.

Symptoms of Bridge Phobia – Fear of bridges:

breathlessness, excessive sweating, nausea, dry mouth, feeling sick, shaking, heart palpitations, inability to speak or think clearly, a fear of dying, becoming mad or losing control, a sensation of detachment from reality or a full blown anxiety attack.

The terror I felt was that I would fall off the edge of a bridge, a road, anything really. I also couldn't go on any amusement park rides, even the smallest kiddy rides during this time. I know it was in my head but I still felt a huge amount of anxiety at the peak of my problem and the fact that it was imagined was very little comfort.

Seattle has a lot of bridges, and I worked in Kirkland, which was a 520 bridge ride away across Lake Washington. I had to cross two bridges each day for work, each way. To go anywhere in Seattle usually meant crossing a bridge of some kind, so I was in a very bad place to have this problem. I knew it was all in my head but that didn't make it easier to face the daily fear of falling off the edge of a bridge, highway, or other surface. I felt betrayed by my own head.

Adventures with Ambien and Other Stories

It took me almost a year before I could cross over Lake Washington without feeling anxiety. It took me over two more years to face and conquer this fear of other bridges. The last time I recall having any sense of panic at all was when I went to cross the Coronado Bridge in San Diego in May of 2003. I could see it in the distance, and the way that it curved reminded me of a roller coaster ride. The curvy nature of the bridge caused instant nausea. I had to pull over and let my mother drive us over the bridge, but after that I was able to drive over it without fear and I now do it all the time. It helped to be in the car, feeling the sway as we drove over it. I was able to look out the window and that was also helpful. Today I can drive across that bridge without any problem. But if you ever experience an uncontrollable reaction to something you will know the helplessness and terror that it can evoke.

I laugh about my phobia—but it isn't really funny. I was truly terrified when my suffering was at its peak. I have a lot more sympathy for others who suffer from any kind of phobia because facing it can cause as much stress as a soldier at war staring down an enemy. I try not to tailgate anyone now because I don't know what the driver in front of me is facing and I don't want to give them more stress.

I think I am cured, but I still feel a little dread when I think of two bridges: The Golden Gate and the Tacoma-Narrows Bridges. I hope I won't have to put my cure to the test on either one but if I ever am faced with having to cross them, I think I can do it today.

Closing a Business

I had worked at my technical writing business for about four years on the side of working a regular job. But when I left Microsoft, I decided I wanted to create my own environment and work full-time for myself. Thus WinPro Online Press was born. I later changed the name to Design Docs, but that is another story.

I had five people working for me at its peak. The day I had been open for three years, we celebrated. Most small businesses close in the first three years. When we stayed open for five years, I was incredibly happy. Unfortunately, my business was one of the many undocumented victims of 9-11-01. I had a lot of small business customers and as they dried up, my business withered on the vine. By April, 2002, I was closing the doors, selling the furniture and saying goodbye to a lovely part of my life. On the way to closing the doors, I had to lay off the people who worked for me, one-by-one. That was the hardest part of being a business owner.

Defending a Name

I was sued for half a million dollars for trademark infringement. WinPro was trademarked by a company in New Jersey and they wanted me to change my name. I originally said I would if they paid for the costs of changing it. I had a huge web site, stationary and a lot of other collateral material with the name WinPro on it. They refused.

I was absolutely terrified to be sued and didn't have the money to pay for an attorney to defend myself. So I decided to do a little research. The first thing I learned is that if someone sues you, you can countersue them for free. So I countered with a million dollar lawsuit. When I looked up the statutes they said I violated, I found they made them up. And, the woman who was suing me was supposed to be a hot shot internet attorney who'd won someone kind of award for being this wonderful attorney. It didn't look good that her company had this million dollar law suit against it.

When the attorney called to talk to me, she said "You don't know who you're messing with little girl." I couldn't let that go without a fight.

Before I'd chosen the name, I'd done some research and I knew about this company. However, they were not using the actual mark on their name and that's why I thought I could use it. So I looked up how to file a complaint with the US Patent and Trademark agency. I filed a complaint about how the company wasn't using their mark and it caused

Lin Laurie

WinPro NJ to have their web site taken down for about 120 days.

When it came time to have a court hearing, it was done by phone. A federal court judge in New Jersey did a conference call. I did have to change my name in the end, but I won all my expenses because they didn't trademark their name correctly and because they made such a sloppy lawsuit. Ms. NJ attorney got bitched out for being nasty to me and the judge threatened to fine her because she was so vile. He wasn't impressed with Ms. Internet Lawyer of the Year at all.

I never want to have to defend myself in court again and don't recommend it but the experience was very time consuming and yet very rewarding.

How to Write a Book in Thirty Days

1. Work on your book for eight months and have most of the material in a first draft state.

2. Commit to having it published by April 15th.

3. Obtain a Twitter account and tweet that your book will be released in April.

4. Create a mailing list and announcement that you send out to all your friends saying the book will be out by mid-April.

5. Have a hard disk crash without having backed up your book.

These are the steps that can inspire someone to an 8-hour a day or 6,000 words per day writing schedule. Exhausting, stressful... Priceless.

I was eventually able to retrieve my lost work but I had to go to a data retrieval specialist and spend nearly a grand to do it. Then I had writer's block and that took some extra time. But here it is. And it is priceless to me.

Adventures of the Orange Red Lipstick

I had heard the legend of a special orange red lipstick and how it mesmerized men and turned them into sexual mushy love slaves before the wearer's eyes. I hadn't believed it really could happen though. I thought it was the invention of someone at MSN News to entice me into reading their insipid Love and Relationship columns or something. Or maybe it was a myth started by some commercial enterprise like Revlon to entice people like me to shove money at them. Wherever it had come from, I had heard that men loved the red orange color more than the blue red shades and if you wore it as makeup or clothing, it caused men to notice.

In the summer of 2003 I had no job, no good prospects and no boyfriend either. I was new to San Diego and I didn't really know anyone except my parents. I needed a pick-me-up and for some reason I decided it would be a new lipstick. I have no idea what called me this option because I don't really believe makeup can dramatically change your outlook in any fundamental way. Also, I've been a red head for more years than I can count and didn't generally go with this shade. Anyhow, I had a notion, followed it into a Macy's store, and ended up with a tube of the bright red orange lipstick and a silly smile on my face.

I forgot I was wearing it as I stopped in at a convenience store to buy some bottled water. I walked into the store, headed right for the rear and had a vague notion someone was staring at me. When I walked up to the register, the man at the counter followed my lips as I said "Hi, and smiled at him." He wasn't focused on my breasts, an area I was used to having men focus on. No, he was looking right below my nose, at my slim thin, red-orange lips. Hmmm, it was interesting that I was getting a little attention from the opposite sex. I felt a little bit of sexual tension; however I wasn't ready to credit the lipstick.

I walked out to my car and noticed that a couple of other men standing outside their truck and drinking sodas seemed to be noticing me. Since I am a plump, middle aged woman of about average looks, I know when I am getting male attention and when I am not (my usual state).

Adventures with Ambien and Other Stories

It was a beautiful day. I applied a fresh coat of lipstick and pinned my hair back. I took the top down on my car and got on the road. Me and my little silver sports car, red hair in the wind, and my bright red orange lips were on a little road trip now.

I passed a very cute biker, riding a Harley sporting a nice bike rider's tan and showing a multitude of tattoos. He was a bad boy, for sure. I liked a little bad in my boys, so to speak, (but not enough to be mistreated) and spent a little time in a racing engine sexual foreplay; first I was a head, then I'd let him get ahead, and then I'd take the lead again. Synchronously crafted like a dance routine, our engines racing wildly as we alternated positions. It was getting hot in here! He tried to flag me to pull over. I sped off, my hair wildly flying in the wind.

Maybe there was something to the myth of the red orange lipstick.

I needed some strings for my mandolin, so I drove to a music store. I wanted to test the waters a little more. I walked in and immediately locked eyes with a gorgeous man who was behind the counter plucking at a guitar. He looked like Tom Sellack during his Magnum PI days. He was very hot, especially for a woman like me who was in a sexual dry spell of some time. I blushed and headed down the rows of sheet music, anxious to get out of site for a minute to regain my composure. My own

Lin Laurie

personal Tom Sellack walked from behind the counter, slowly getting closer. I walked faster. I noticed my breath was a little ragged and I could feel a red flush slowly creeping up my face. Damn! I was probably perspiring. I hoped I wasn't hot flashing too.

"Hi, can I help you?"

"No thanks. I just need mandolin strings."

"They're in the back," he pointed. He walked down the row ahead of mine, keeping pace with me. I was extremely interested in him now.

I averted my eyes, trying not to trip, and headed for the strings. I found the ones I wanted, and turned around quickly. He was right behind me. Hot and sneaky. What a combination! I was very attracted.

"Sorry," he said as I walked into him.

We chatted about nothing as we walked toward the front counter. As he rang me up, he asked me my name. Then he invited me to a bluegrass jam, where I could meet other musicians, and get the opportunity to play music with others.

I walked out smiling. He had my number and he called me that night. We went out that weekend and kept dating for three months. He was fascinated by my ability and interest in playing the mandolin and we spent many evenings talking about instruments, music, and our favorite songs. I nicknamed him the Mandolin Maniac. He was my transition man. I was transitioning from Seattle to San Diego, and a new life. I was very excited about the future after meeting him. Meeting him gave me hope that my new life would be different and more exciting than it had been for the last ten years in Seattle. I wanted a little passion and fun and I thought the Maniac might be my ticket to some of that juicy life.

Somewhere along the line, I lost the guy and the orange red lipstick. But I still have hope that the juicy life I wanted to create was somewhere down here, close to the border. I haven't found just the right color of lipstick since then, and haven't found the right man either. But you know, I have a networking conference coming up and I think I will make another stab at finding another tube of lipstick. I need a new boyfriend. I am tired of being alone.

By the way, I ran into the Maniac recently. He'd grayed a lot and seemed to age a lot after turning 50. I think the real Tom Sellack was looking much better these days. Isn't it funny how people you were once attracted to seem shorter and heavier when you see them after time has gone by?

Lin Laurie

My Neighbor was Probably a Serial Killer

We lived on a cul de sac when I was growing up. One the east side was a family of four—the Cramers. There was Wayne, the father, Martha, the mother, Barbara, the oldest girl (about 18), and the youngest—Wayne Jr, who was about ten years younger than his sister. Wayne and Martha were in his their mid-forties when they had their second child. He was a mid-life mistake, and they let everyone know how they felt about him by calling him Booboo.

Wayne senior was a mean man who would force Booboo to help him whenever he was home. Senior would catch fish and make him behead them, he would drink whiskey and berate Booboo on the job he was doing. Sometimes he would smack Booboo around. He would call Booboo all kinds of names, the likes of which we never heard in our house.

Booboo Craddock was a horrid child. We had a plastic, above ground swimming pool in our back yard. He would hammer nails into boards so that the point stuck through and he'd throw them over the fence into our pool. He nearly hit me one time, so I am certain he was the one doing it.

He also used to catch frogs, electrocute them from the wires that crossed over our yards, and then he would use the dead frogs like cards and attach them to the wheels of his bike so they would make horrible sounds when he pedaled around.

He would capture any kind of bug and squish it with his bare hands. He would capture pets and torture them. We were always making sure our cats were in at night so he wouldn't get his hands on them.

No one at school liked Booboo. He didn't try at all to make friends and everything that he did was strange, even to young boys looking for adventure. My brothers, who seemed to accept just about anyone, would not touch Booboo with a ten foot pole. With all the curiosity young boys had, they were never curious enough to hang with Booboo. So he went around alone, no one would eat lunch with him, no one would talk to him unless made to do so.

The Cramers had a very nice front yard covered in some sort of expensive grass. We were always told not to walk on the grass. Anytime we were playing in the cul de sac Mrs. Cramer would come out and warn us not to play on the grass. Then she would stand inside her house watching us through the window. No one wanted to go on that lawn. We were all scared of the Cramers.

One time we were playing dodge ball and the ball ended up on the Cramers lawn. It was like a slice of life that occurred in slow motion. We were all paralyzed watching the ball roll up on the lawn and stop, right in the middle of the yard. As soon as the ball rolled to a stop, Mrs. Cramer opened the door of her house and walked out, wearing a pink house coat, and with her hair in curlers. She had a cigarette hanging from her mouth and a large butcher knife clutched in her hand. She strode with purpose to the middle of her yard and plunged the knife into the ball. For a moment it remained poised on the tip of the knife while she held it high. Then she shook the ball off the knife tip and we watched it bounce, thud, thud, thud back to the street where it lay dead. She killed our ball. Every child watching was left watching in horror with their mouths open.

Booboo started lighting fires in his early teens. He burnt down his father's boat and part of the garage. We'd moved by then and were no longer his neighbors. Maybe his father's drinking and treatment contributed to the person he turned out to be. I don't know. What I do know is that he had at least two of the three issues that most serial killers have. They call it the serial killer triumvirate and it is bed wetting (after 12), fire starting, and animal torture.

I feel like I grew up next to the Bates home and the Cramers were the Bates family. I know some day I will hear that he turned into a serial killer. His childhood was horrible enough that I can't imagine him turning out to be anything else. I'm sure his parents are long gone by now, but I still wonder what they were thinking to call him Booboo?

Dead Fred

At the age of twenty-eight, I recall walking into a room full of people—mostly men—and first seeing Fred. He was a beautiful man, with a natural gorgeous bronze tan, bright blue eyes, and copper streaks in his light brown, curly hair. He looked like some of the more handsome Jesus pictures I'd seen hanging on the walls of my devout Catholic friends.

My first thoughts were *"Oh my."* And then I thought, *"Not my type,"* but what a gorgeous man.

He pursued me, subtly at first, by asking first for my name, then by starting to get to know me better. He was sweet, gentle, and totally hot. We started going for walks, talking like friends, and I didn't think he was interested in me in any other way but I was wrong. We both fell in love very quickly.

Unfortunately, he also had a side I didn't see, but that would ultimately influence both our lives. He suffered from major depression and was suicidal. He was the kind of suicidal person who never said anything and just one day was here and the next was gone.

Lin Laurie

One Friday night he didn't come home. By the next morning I was looking everywhere for him. Eventually the San Diego Police called me.

"Do you know Fred S___?"

"Yes, I've been looking for him since yesterday." I was frantic and my voice quivered in fear.

"Well, he's dead."

There was no "I'm sorry," or "condolences" or any kind of sympathetic comment. I have never understood how someone could announce another's death like that. I hope they've had a little sensitivity training since then.

The night before Fred died he picked a fight with me. I could see that's what it was and didn't understand what he was doing, but I was suspicious that something was up. In the morning he took the car keys and left me a note that looked on the surface like an apology for the fight. In retrospect, it was his suicide note.

Fred had taken a garden hose and attached it to the exhaust pipe of his car, put the hose through the window and asphyxiated on the fumes. A security guard found him behind a bank building in downtown San Diego. He must have felt so terrible and alone to do this to himself.

Adventures with Ambien and Other Stories

I was devastated. I can't tell you the hell that was dealing with day-to-day business like returning the car he used to the owner, or having to track down his final paycheck to pay rent with. People have to survive and they have to grieve; but the business of life goes on regardless.

During this time I was in conflict with his mother about whether I could see him and say goodbye and about where he wanted to be buried. It was a horrible time. I left San Diego within four days and didn't return for six years. I could not stop crying for months after his death and I am still sad when I think of the waste he made of his life.

I went into therapy immediately because I knew there was a large danger that I would take on a sense of guilt about his death. I never did feel guilty, but I just felt betrayed and sad that he would take the chicken's way out of life. I had no idea he was so weak. It was a stupid waste of a potentially great human being.

I used to wonder if someone were playing a joke on me and that he was still alive. That's what happens when you can't hold someone's hand and say goodbye to them. My mind went through a lot in those days and I know some of it could have been avoided if his mother had let me see his body. But she wouldn't do it. She thought she was protecting me. She was wrong.

Lin Laurie

There must really be something wrong with me that I did not for a single second recognize Fred's desperation or that he would or could take his own life. I decided around that time that there was no way I would ever fall in love again. Love hurt way too much to ever risk feeling it again.

My subconscious made a decision at that time. I don't sleep—insomnia is ever present in my life. I'm not sure if it is my mind's way of trying to be hyper-vigilant to protect me or if Fred's death stressed me out so much that I have a very difficult time sleeping to this day. The insomnia comes and goes depending on what else is going on in my life, but this is the event that first led me into a search for peace at night and is part of what led me to use Ambien.

Bundles of Boobs

I am all for plastic surgery, fillers, tummy tucks, boob jobs, etc. I figure if God gave us the knowledge to make ourselves a little prettier as we age, we have the money to spend on it, we want it for ourselves, we should do it. But no one should force you to have the boob job of their dreams.

Plastic surgery should be something you want for yourself since you are the one who has to endure the pain of it and also deal with the after effects of your decision. Boyfriends might come and go, but you will be dying with those boobs on so you'd better really like them. And, if you feel you have to change everything about the way you look, or to resemble someone completely different from how you were born, seek therapy. Surgery is no way to learn to like yourself.

I have great breasts. I didn't always feel that way about my breasts. I grew up with about a 36 D, and never felt inferior in that area. I actually felt they were too large because I developed them in the 6th grade and they drew a lot of unwanted attention my way. As I got older and gravity took its toll they were a little less perky and I thought it would be nice to someday get them adjusted so they aimed a little higher, or, maybe even pointed to the stars. But it wasn't an overriding passion, just a passing thought.

One day, I found myself at a plastic surgeon's office so they could check some rosacea I was developing on my cheeks. While I was waiting, they handed me a book of before and after shots of women who had had their boobs done. I didn't spend a lot of time looking at naked women, so it was a revelation to see how they looked and how they could be changed for the better. Breasts became pretty interesting to me at that moment.

Lin Laurie

When the nurse called my name, and she saw me looking at the book, she asked, "Would you like to touch them and see how they feel?"

"What do you mean?" I felt a wave of fear and anxiety coming over me at the idea of touching another woman's breasts.

"Some of us have had them done and we act as models for our patients to see. It's nothing really."

"I couldn't."

"It's perfectly fine. If you come with me, you can touch mine." She headed back toward the door of a small room. Once inside, she pulled up her shirt and showed me her boobs.

It was the first time in my life I had ever looked directly at the areolas of another woman's breasts. They were beautiful. Really beautiful. High and perky. I wanted them. I wanted to be the bearer of boobs that looked like hers.

"Go ahead. Touch them." I felt face to face with a huge taboo. I couldn't. I shouldn't. You had to be a lesbian to touch women's breasts. However, I did. I reached out with my forefinger and pressed it into her saline-filled flesh. It felt awesome. I knew in that moment I wanted my own boob job. Talk about an up sale! I was hooked on the titular dream. And I didn't want to get them for anyone else but myself.

However, before I plunked down the $3500 to have them raised and enriched, I wanted to do a little research. The doctor had said he'd recommend I go bigger and get a little lift. I hadn't thought about changing the size of my breast line and I realized it was a huge commitment. Clothes would forever look differently. In fact, a lot of my pre-boob job clothing had to be given away as it just wouldn't fit. Anyhow, I decided I needed to do some research before I decided on the size issue.

Where does one go to discuss boob jobs with other women? You can't just poll women at work and find a gaggle of boobs. A bundle of breasts, couple of cleavage enhancements, you get the idea. So after thinking about it, and being influenced by the Bada Bing of The Sopranos fame, I decided a trip to a strip joint was the answer. I wasn't brave enough to venture out on my own to a strip club. I got a writer friend to accompany me on a research mission. He said he wanted to know about them for his book, but I happened to have read parts of his book and it barely featured any women, so I was a little skeptical, but also desperate to have someone come with me. He drove over and we went in. I don't know if it was women's night, but they let me in for free.

A strip club is as dehumanizing as I'd expected it would be. But that's all I expected. We sat down and ordered drinks, and began to watch the show.

Lin Laurie

A woman wearing a plaid skirt that reminded me of Catholic school uniforms, was up first. She was surprisingly flat chested given that the focus was all about the breasts. At least that's what I thought the focus would be. After she did her dance, she left the stage and began to work the audience. When she got to us, we told her we were doing research and my friend tipped her. She got friendlier as we talked, and promised to tell the other girls about me. Eventually, she walked away and spent hardly any time with the single men in the audience.

As each girl came out, I noticed they seemed to be featured by order of the size of their breasts. The first ones were small breasted, and as time went on, the boobs got bigger. We talked to each one. I found out the following:

- Many of them had gotten multiple surgeries
- All of them went bigger with each surgery
- Bigger boobs equated to more money in the strip club business

I decided that I didn't want huge boobs as I wasn't planning to be a stripper, so while that was good information, it didn't make me want the mega boobs. Besides, working around a lot of men in an office all day, I didn't want that much attention on them. I just wanted a little spring in my cleavage, that's all. Not freak city.

I also learned that if you have them inserted beneath your chest muscles, they take longer to sag and that this was the preferred way. However, it hurt more and took longer to heal.

One of the women offered me a free lap dance that night. I didn't really understand why she would or what it would do for me, so I declined. My friend was disappointed because he wasn't offered one, and he didn't get to see me get one. He eventually got over it. At least I believe so. We eventually parted ways.

One good thing that came from that visit was an increase in my own sense of my body. I realized that those girls, although younger and probably cuter, and absolutely thinner, didn't have anything really that I didn't have. There was no secret dance that they did to hypnotize men. They just got naked so men could look at them. I'd pierced the veil on strippers and learned some new respect for my own body.

The Aftermath...

I started to wear some inserts to adjust my size upward and so it wouldn't be such a shock when I got mine done. In April of 2005 I got a severance check from my employer due to a massive layoff. This gave me the time to have the surgery and to heal, as well as the money to afford it. And even better, I wouldn't be returning to an office full of men who would have noticed the size increase.

What is really interesting to me is that I feel less a sense of ownership about my breasts now, than I did before two foreign objects were placed in my chest. I can actually pick up my shirt and show them off proudly; this is not something I'd have done before. I just don't care as much or am not as modest about them now, not that I'm showing them off whenever and wherever I go.

I am now a 38 DD. They are indeed awesome and I get to touch them whenever I want without fear of turning into a lesbian.

Thank You Ford Motors

I worked on the assembly line when I was eighteen, in 1974. Ford Motors had a plant in Milpitas, CA and I was extremely pleased to get on there. The pay was about a little more than double the minimum wage (I made about $3.75 a hour) and my friends were extremely envious.

Every day, I would walk about half way through the plant to my position on the assembly line amid cat calls from the men on the line. It was intimidating, but also comforting. I was eighteen, had long hair, was pretty thin, and looked pretty good.

Adventures with Ambien and Other Stories

My job was to put the safety reflectors on the driver's side of Pintos and Mustangs. The guy next to me was one of the Hells Angels, but he was very nice for a cursing, drug using, motorcyclist. He handed me parts from a tall shelf whenever I ran out, and tried to help me as much as he could. However, every other word out of his mouth was "F***".

"Let me f***in' get that for ya." He'd say and hand me new parts. Thoughtful.

I have never left a job each afternoon, where I was so tired that I could barely make it home and to bed. After the first two days, I noticed my dreams were all starting to come at me as if they were on the assembly line. Out of the corner of my eye, the room seemed to be moving the same way. I think that working on a moving line was affecting my brain.

At the end of the first week, when I walked in that Friday morning, they told me that I had only been doing half of my job and I needed to pick up the other half (the piece the Hells Angel had been doing). They handed me a drill that was longer than my arm and told me to start putting the reflectors in and then screwing them in with the drill. I left a lot of reflectors on the top of cars that morning. I couldn't physically do the job and I didn't understand why they gave me such an impossible task. At lunch time, I did the most horrible thing I could do as an assembly-line worker—I walked off the line.

I went home that day and immediately looked into college. I knew I never wanted to have a physical job again as a way of making a living. If I went to college I would be guaranteed jobs that were physically much easier. I could sit on my ass—I would just have to use my brain more.

Note: At 1 pm on the day I walked off the line, my stepfather's friend, who worked in Ford's QA department, walked out to pick me off the line. He'd just heard I was working there and was going to pull me into a cushier job. Had that happened, I may have spent many years at Ford until the factory closed sometime in the 1990's. It's funny sometimes how things work out.

Running Away

When I was about five, I used to love to watch three programs on Sunday night:

- Car 54
- Bonanza
- Alfred Hitchcock Presents

Many times my mother would let me watch them. I think Alfred Hitchcock Presents ended at 10 pm so that was pretty late for a five-year old to stay up on a Sunday night.

One night my mother decided I couldn't stay up. It made me so mad that I decided I'd run away from home. I made sure my announcement was dramatic.

"Mother, I am leaving home if you won't let me watch TV."

"OK. Let me help you. I'll get you a suitcase." She walked upstairs and brought down a small suitcase and plopped it down in front of me.

Stunned, I grabbed some clothing out of my dresser drawer and threw it into the suitcase. By now, my brother Rick was watching from his room as I zipped up my bag.

My mother went to the front door and opened it. I think that was the first time I realized I had talked myself into a corner and if I didn't go through with what I said, it would somehow change the kind of person I was.

I walked through the front door. My brother ran down the hall and said, "I want to go." He was dragging an empty suitcase behind him.

Lin Laurie

My mother held the door open for him and as he walked outside with me, she closed the door behind her.

It is very dark when you are a five-year old standing on a dark front porch with a suitcase and a four-year old. I still believed in the boogey man and was terrified but didn't want to show it.

I tried dragging the suitcase from the porch to the sidewalk. I had no plan except to get off of the porch. The suitcase was too heavy and I could barely move it. My apprehension increased as I imagined I saw eyes peering at us through the trees that surrounded our house. In that moment, I felt defeat as I knew I wasn't really running away. I realized I had no place to go. I think it was in this moment that I learned I could be stubborn and yet I knew I would not win.

"Can we go in?" my brother asked.

"No."

"It's dark out here," he whined.

"Let's just sit out here for a while. Look, try to catch a firefly." I thought if I distracted him I could make my fight for independence last longer.

We stayed in the dark, sitting on the porch for a very long time. I'm sure it wasn't long at all, but just seemed like it was. I did see my mother peek out of the curtains to check on us. Eventually she opened the door and let us back in. I walked up the stairs to my bedroom, saddened by the fact that the first time I'd tried to get my own way I'd tanked out. There would be many other times to come where it would happen again. I wouldn't be who I am though, if I didn't try.

Sticking Up for the Underdog

West Caldwell, New Jersey was a small town that was just a short train ride away from New York City. Sometime around my 5th or 6th year of life, a family of Pakistanis moved to town. One of their children, Udoh, attended school with me.

To this very day, I do not understand prejudice and the anger and ugly actions it creates. I befriended Udoh, and we would walk home to my house after school each day. We'd sit on the front porch and talk about his life and how different it was from mine. I was fascinated by the differences between our lives and kept asking about his life.

To others in town, my behavior was appalling. I was causing a scandal in a small town at a very young age. Eventually, my mother wouldn't let me talk or play with him any longer and soon after that they left town. I remember a lot of ugly talk about the family. I also remember my mother trying to stick up for my right to talk to whomever I wanted. But she was overcome by community resistance and it took me many years to understand why.

This is another example of an event that shaped the person I am today. I am truly fascinated by people of other cultures and I love to listen to stories of their lives. I strongly resent anyone trying to talk to me about who I can and cannot befriend. I hate to listen to anyone who speaks words of prejudice and I find that most people who try to tell me that I am better than another person because of the color of my skin is really someone terrified by the differences. Prejudice stems from fear and ignorance; both are qualities I do not admire and am saddened by.

The Eighth Brother

After my mother had seven children she swore she would not have any more children. I was twelve by this time and really tired of having to take care of her kids. I loved my brothers but I'd spent the last six years taking care of one or more of them. I wanted some time to myself. I was sooo selfish.

So my mother swore on a stack of bibles that she would not have any more children. And time went on and she didn't.

One afternoon, when I got home from school my stepfather took me into my bedroom and closed the door. He wanted to talk to me about something and by his actions I could tell it was important. He sat me down and explained that my mother was pregnant again. Do you know the picture of the man who wants to scream by Edvard Munch? They model the Scary Movie masks on his pictures. I didn't know about those images back then, but I looked like that man in my head. I wanted to scream so badly.

I told my stepfather that I wanted to run away. But as soon as I said it, I realized that at the age of twelve there was nothing I could do to make a living and it would be impossible to live on the streets. I had no concept of what could really happen to me on the streets but I knew I wouldn't have a place to sleep or anything to eat and that's all it took.

We'd just seen something on TV about all the young people being compelled to runaway to San Francisco and I remembered seeing shots of kids not much older than me, hugging together under a single blanket living on the streets and I knew that wasn't for me. I knew I had to stay but I didn't have to be happy about it and I wasn't. And not only was I mad about it but I made sure everyone else knew I was unhappy. That was the first time I realized I had a tiny bit of power in my family because if they weren't worried about my reaction they wouldn't have told me like that. My mother would have been the one to tell me.

Lin Laurie

They'd hid it from me as long as they could, but my mother was about six months along when they realized they couldn't put it off any longer. I hadn't noticed that she had gained weight but it seemed like within days of hearing about it, she suddenly looked pregnant.

My youngest brother was born in July of that year. His name would be Zachary (for Dr. Zachary Smith on "Lost in Space") or Zeke if it weren't for me. I talked my parents into naming him Robin so that we could call him Rob, as I had a crush on Rob on "My Three Sons." He hasn't been nearly grateful enough for my participation in his naming.

Gaining Power

I felt pretty powerless growing up in a family of boys. My mother made me do all of the chores while my brother did absolutely nothing except to clean their own rooms. I really did sometimes feel like I was treated like a slave.

On Thanksgiving 1970, I'd helped my mother cook dinner and put it on the table. After we'd eaten, she told me to get up and do the dishes. I had to do dishes all the time but the pots and pans needed for a holiday feast were way outside the norm and I got mad.

"You never make the boys doing anything! They aren't helpless, why can't they do something?" I was trembling, I was so mad and they'd tripped a switch in me. I was tired of doing everything.

And so it was written, on Thanksgiving Day, 1970 that my brothers would take turns doing dishes, doing all the yard work, and taking care of their own clothing. I was no longer the family slave. I was learning the power of my own anger. The weirdest thing about that day was that I didn't have to threaten; I didn't have to do anything but express my feelings and things changed.

Psychosomatic 101

One of the things I was always required to do was to take care of the yard. I would always argue about this because I already was responsible for taking care of cleaning the house, helping my brothers with their homework, and doing laundry.

For some reason, I didn't mind mowing the lawn. I liked the smell of the fresh cut grass and our front lawn wasn't very large. The backyard was fairly good sized and I did mind having to mow it.

We had a large raised bed in one part of the back yard that was full of weeds. One day my mother ordered me to go back there and pull the weeds. I didn't want to do it and I groused, but I did go out and start pulling them. After a few minutes of pulling, I started to feel funny. My arms were red and blotches started to appear, and I was having a difficult time breathing as well.

I ended up going to the hospital and getting a shot of Benadryl. Eventually the swelling and the hives went away, but I was never asked to pull weeds or do yard work again. I strongly believe in a mind-body connection and think I created that allergy because I was so mad.

Running Away Through Life

I was a teenage runaway. I left my home several times while I was a minor to get away from the unhappiness I felt living with my seven brothers. Eventually I was able to move out legally and live on my own before I was eighteen. I understand why I did it, what I was unhappy about, and I've come a very long way emotionally since that time. But some recent reflections have caused me to look at that behavior and how it has rippled through my life and affected my relationships.

My mom and stepdad were yellers and damaged a lot of property in the first ten years of their relationship. They threw things, broke possessions, and generally created great disturbances when they fought. So that's what I learned to do. In early relationships I acted out what I knew how to do when I was angry. But I didn't like the ugly feelings that came up when I did that so eventually I matured. I actually have to leave if I end up in a room with a family of yellers. It affected me a lot later on down the line. To this day, if I walk into a family of loudly communicating people, my first urge is to run out of the room. I truly hate loud arguments and you will very rarely see me lose my temper enough to participate in one.

In my twenties I lived with a handsome English man of Italian descent. Conrad was about twenty-eight, and came to the US to learn to fly. Apparently, in England the landing fees for Heathrow were so expensive for private planes that it was much more cost-effective to move to the US to learn to pilot. He wanted to become a commercial pilot and so his father gave him the money to live in the US while he took flying lessons.

We didn't fight often, but the first time we did fight, he didn't speak to me for three days. He gave me the complete, absolute silent treatment. This was totally unfamiliar behavior to me and I was floored. I cried, I asked my friends, I went slowly crazy. We reconciled and things were great for a few months, but then it happened again.

In therapy, they tell you to do something different from the way you normally behave and see what that does to the behavior of others. It's kind of like the Newton's law of motion: that every action has an equal and opposite reaction. I was prepared for his behavior this time. I knew that what he was doing to me was purposefully hurtful behavior, I didn't like how he withdrew, and I reacted much differently the second time.

Silent treatment is funny. You don't know you're getting it until you try to engage someone in conversation because they are being so quiet. So when I finally did that, I figured that he was just waiting for me to try to say something. He didn't comment on what I said. So I said, "Oh, it's silent treatment time again."

Nothing.

"What do you want for dinner?"

He said nothing.

"Oh, I guess I can fix whatever I want since you aren't talking to me." I went and fixed dinner. It was something he didn't particularly like. He quietly ate it, never once looking me dead in the eyes.

In the morning, I was at it again.

"Do you want some tea?" He usually wanted tea every morning.

He said more of nothing.

"Well, I am making tea with two tea bags. You can fix it the way you want." I started heating the water for the tea.

"I'm making oatmeal. Do you want some?"

Again, nothing.

"I guess you can't say so I'll let you fix your own breakfast." I had my back to him and I smiled. I was actually starting to enjoy the game.

It went on like that a little longer and then he got tired of being forced to do things he didn't want to do and he started talking to me. We went from three days of silent treatment to about one day by the second time he pulled that crap. This was a huge improvement and it taught me a lot about dealing with people who tried to punish you when they don't like your behavior. He tried to do it a couple of additional times but it never lasted very long and he slowly realized that it wasn't working with me. I still laugh when I think about those days.

He was a lot of fun. We would take plane trips to San Jose and pick up one or another of my brothers for the weekend or we'd take the plane and land at a small airport, call a restaurant and have them pick us up and have a wonderful dinner. I started taking unlogged flying lessons with him and overcame a fear of flying that I'd had most of my life.

Lin Laurie

Another time, he made me so mad that I took all his flight books and threw them on the front yard. I remember papers flying out from the binders and it was oddly satisfying. I also remember him running around the yard to pick them up. After that experience we lived together pretty harmoniously for the rest of our relationship. It lasted until he got his private pilot's license and then he returned to England. He asked me to visit but I never did. I had a sense that if I did go over there, he'd be in control and have the advantage, being a native. I let him go, but I missed the fun we had once he was gone.

In my early thirties I married a big man. He was over six feet tall and very solid. When he got angry and yelled at me, I would actually shake. I responded by quietly writing up a list of things to say so I would stay focused and not utter anything in anger that would haunt me or hurt him. I cannot tell you how much he hated that I did that. And I admit years after this marriage ended, that I gave him plenty to be mad at me about. I was not the best wife and I totally didn't meet his expectations. Then again, he didn't meet mine. But it is sad when any marriage ends.

In my defense, he didn't tell me he wanted to have kids or adopt them and to do some of the things I'd known my whole life that I didn't want to do. Oops! You really need to be honest in your relationships or you can end up with someone very different from what you want. Anyhow, that marriage didn't last long and I will take the lion's share of the blame for its destruction.

Now, in looking back, all of the times I didn't agree with friends, lovers, family, I had a habit of withdrawing from interaction with them until I could come to terms with what they wanted or a compromise was reached. That didn't seem like bad behavior to me at the time, because it kept me from horrible arguments with others. After all, you can't argue with someone when they just aren't there. Physically I was there but my mind, my emotions, and my attention were not. If I didn't want to play, I would take my emotional baggage and go to my emotional home. I thought I was protecting myself from hurt but really I was just withdrawing from the play and that's not right.

I can't say I am great at conflict resolution today but I still don't like yelling matches and I tend to talk instead of fight. I think this is better behavior and the people that I relate to seem fine with it but I think relationships evolve and grow and I may find a better way to deal with anger and upset tomorrow.

My rules for my friends today are:

1. Never argue when drinking. It is not productive to argue with people under the influence of something.

Lin Laurie

2. Make sure you are arguing over the same thing. Sometimes I've found that I'm mad about something completely different than my friend is upset over.

3. Leave history in the past. Just because someone did something yesterday, it doesn't mean they will do it today.

4. Say things like "I really like that you do/are…"

5. Use statements like "I feel like…" These statements make people feel like you aren't stuck in blame. If you want to blame someone, you aren't ready to work something out with them.

6. Acknowledge people for the contribution they are to your life. This one is a killer and has caused me to have some wonderful relationship breakthroughs.

Recently, in a conversation with my current boyfriend, I used all of these rules and we ended up having a huge emotionally charged talk that ended up with the best, A-game, hooting and hollering sex we ever had. So this way does work for me. It also encourages me to think that you can have the same boyfriend for many years and still have experiences like that. I am hoping for many more of those experiences and so is he!

Each man in my life ended up leaving in some way or the relationship ended. But the relationships have been getting better as I get older and deal with my problems.

Reality TV vs. Reality Life

I am not a big watcher of reality television by any means but there are a couple of voyeuristic opportunities that have called to me.

Breaking Bonaduce

Danny Bonaduce is well known as Danny Partridge of Partridge Family fame. He grew up on TV, getting whatever he wanted, and he turned into a very troubled adult TV and radio personality.

Watching his reality TV show is like watching a train wreck about to happen. This show only lasted a couple of seasons before Danny self-destructs on camera, ruins his long-time marriage, and goes on a big binge of drug usage and drinking.

Danny reminds me of one of my brothers. Danny talks like him, looks a lot like him, and except for the ability to live on a budget far above a normal man's he has that wild, bad boy lifestyle like my brother does. My brother ended up in prison. I hope Danny manages to get his self-destructive behavior under control before they become roommates.

I wonder if the fascination is with Danny is the same as what draws one to a traffic accident. We don't want to look at the bloody scene, but we can't look away either. I also feel like I am hearing my brother when I hear him speak so there is some comfort there.

Every so often I search the internet to see where Danny is now. I loved his radio show and I would still listen if I could. I guess I am just one of those people...

Celebrity Rehab with Dr. Drew

What a great idea! Let's watch famous addicts sabotage their lives and fall from grace. Watch them walk around high or kicking drugs, and suffering to find what is real in phony Hollywood. Some of them drool, can't function at all, and are emotionally and physically disabled. Fascinating.

In season 1, Jeff Conway (Taxi) drives up to rehab drunk off his ass or high on drugs; I'm not sure which addiction he suffered from, but obviously he had a problem. He is very forthcoming about what he is and how he got that way. He also enters rehab so high that he can barely talk and he needs a wheel chair to get around. In viewing other episodes, this seems to be a typical way people show up for rehab. They do their drug of choice "one last time" and walk in high. It's a shame, but if it works to get them there, then I'm all for that.

A female wrestler denies having any problem and can't understand why she's in rehab even though in the background the show televises videos of her drinking and falling down. Didn't she agree to come? How come she doesn't know why she's there?

Sometimes family, close friends, and management enable addicts not out of love, but because it makes them easier to manage or manipulate. You see a lot of that going on here. Some of these people are perceived, if not actually well-off by many standards, and the drugs allow them access and power over an addict. Once the addict starts to respond to treatment, the relative or significant other tries to 'help' them by bringing in drugs or helping them escape.

Denial, dysfunction, and bad dressing seem to be recurring themes. Rudeness, entitlement, spoiled brats, lots of bad language—these are expected behaviors. And everyone seems to smoke as a way to get through their addictive behaviors.

You don't have to be rich or famous to be an addict. Many poor, uneducated people use drugs to mask their lack of opportunities. Housewives do it out of boredom, truckers do it to stay awake on long hauls, and writers do it to overcome insomnia. There are a million reasons why and a million drugs, legal or not, to make you crave them. Today I heard they are selling 'bath salts' as the latest drug. If you want to live in a cotton candy phase, feeling as little as possible, there is something out there for you.

Lin Laurie

One of my favorite seasons was the third one. Dennis Rodman, Heidi Fleiss, Mackenzie Phillips, Mike Starr, Tom Sizemore, and a few others were there to get clean and sober.

Heidi and Tom Sizemore had a violent history and he actually went to jail for physically abusing her. I was shocked that they ended up in the same place at the same time, but it was interesting to watch sparks fly. I happen to be a Tom Sizemore fan and he was the reason I started to watch the show in the first place.

Mike Starr was the original bassist for the band Alice in Chains and was heroin-tortured as well as addicted to pain killers and anything else he could get his hands on. His suffering made for interesting viewing. He was rude, he was obnoxious, and he was another train wreck walking. He had been in 30 previous drug rehabs and didn't seem to have much hope of staying clean. Amazingly, he did end up getting clean and appeared to stay clean in the reunion episode shot the following season. I'm never sure if I'm watching the real thing or if they captured someone, cleaned them up, and pointed a TV camera in their face, not caring if they are promoting a lie or not. I like to think that Dr. Drew wouldn't condone that behavior, but I don't know for sure.

Adventures with Ambien and Other Stories

I am addicted to Celebrity Rehab. I was online last night looking for when the next season would start. I don't like everyone who attends, but I can't stop watching. When things happen like Gary Busey showing up for his stint thinking he was hired on to help people stay straight, well it is just something I need to watch.

Note: Mike Starr, 44, was found dead from an assumed drug overdose in March of 2011. I'm sad for him and for his family. Drug abuse is a tragedy that ruins many lives and causes addicts' families extensive suffering. I am sad to hear that another life has been taken and that Mike couldn't find the strength to overcome his disease.

Further note: Jeff Conway died on May 27th, 2011 at the age of 61 of pneumonia associated with drug addiction.

Being Still

During the fall of 2010, I spent a lot of time alone and depressed. I had a difficult time doing anything and could barely get dressed in the morning. My cat that I had for 19 ½ years died and I was very much alone in an empty house.

Outside one morning I noticed that there were larger rocks mixed in with smaller rocks along my flower borders. I'd live in the same house over seven years without this site bothering me but for some reason I felt compelled to separate them.

I dug small white rocks and holding two or three in my hands, I carried them to a white rock collection point. I did this until my back was hurting and I could no longer stand without pain.

Subsequently, I worked at this task a little at a time. I felt I had a purpose every time I went outside and I couldn't rest in my hammock or water my yard until I'd done a few rocks each day. I remembered the African proverb, "How does an ant eat an elephant? And the answer: "One bite at a time."

One rock at a time. I started to think back over my life at this approach to other things I'd accomplished. These were all things that had more importance attached to them than the moving of rocks. I used to develop custom financial applications for a living; creating something functional where before there had been nothing. When I started, I didn't know an accounts payable system from payroll or a debit from a credit. But slowly I learned. As a baby learns to walk one step at a time, I learned to program, one byte of knowledge at a time. And I remembered how pleased I was with myself whenever a new piece of knowledge stuck to something previous, thus building context.

Adventures with Ambien and Other Stories

Eventually I finished programming one system, then another, and I learned about accounting, winery applications, and how to do job costing in the construction industry. I learned to analyze systems and to figure things out when I didn't know how to do something. I developed confidence.

I thought back to the first book I'd ever written. It was a 117 page fax user guide. When I started, I thought I could write but I really wasn't sure. I knew in theory I could do anything I set my mind to, so with a positive attitude, I built that book word by word, task by task. After I would write a page or so I'd get up and reward myself with candy. Eventually, I had my first writing sample—one of hundreds that I would write over the years—but one that I was so pleased with initially because it proved to me that I could actually make a living as a writer. At the same time, I weighed out of that job at about fifteen pounds more than when I'd started.

I could write a book!

All the while, when I was picking up this knowledge, I was building context for my life but all I knew at the time was that I was learning how to do something that kept my mind engaged, kept me busy, and helped me build a since of confidence and pride in my job.

Lin Laurie

We don't start out knowing anything. If breathing were not a natural function, none of us would know how to draw a breath. But we learn—to eat, to get along, and eventually how to love ourselves and others. And now here I was in my fifties, having to learn about myself all over again, as though I'd had amnesia and woken up without a memory of who I was and what I loved.

At that moment, all I knew for sure is that I had a back yard full of rocks that are mixed together and I'd like to sort them out while I have time, even if the only one who is satisfied with my little task is me.

The yard is coming along quite nicely. The rocks are sorted and displayed in a way that pleases me although my gardener keeps messing some of them up. And now I know that I can survive a horribly deep depression and crazy times even if it means I do things that don't make sense to other people.

I Forgot My Boyfriend's Name

One day, while sitting with a group of people, waiting for a class to start, someone new came to our table that only I knew. I started to introduce them to the others at the table. When I got to my boyfriend's name, I looked at him dead in the eye and my mind went completely blank. I absolutely could not recall his name. Being that it was Bob, the simplest name in existence and also the name of one of my brothers, I felt horrible. He finally helped me by introducing himself. I cannot tell you the weirdness of the stare he gave me that day or how horrible I felt.

I tell this story because I was also diagnosed with Adult Attention Deficit Disorder (AADD). It all started when I went to my regular doctor for a routine checkup. She asked me a few questions, and based on my answers referred me to a doctor specializing in AADD. If you've ever taken one of these tests, you will know that there isn't any time perspective on them. When they ask if you've ever felt restless in class, or day dreamed, they don't take into consideration that yes, everyone does at some point, and if you've managed to make it to your forties without problems, then it likely isn't serious.

Had I ever procrastinated on anything—of course I have. Who hasn't? So having written over 250 user guides, and developed an unknown number of projects during my professional life, I was diagnosed with AADD and put on medication.

At first I just trusted that my doctor was right and I should take this medication. If there was ever a medication made for cleaning house, some of the medications they give you to combat AADD are miracle workers. I attacked tasks like a whirling dervish, lost a ton of weight, and was wildly hungry when the pills wore off. If that had been all that happened, I would probably still be taking them. But when they began to interfere with my memory, I had to stop.

I have to wonder how many children are falsely diagnosed so that they are quieted in class by the medications. Are we stripping our children of natural energy because classes can't handle their exuberance? Based on my experience, I have to wonder... I also have to wonder how much of this ADHD stuff is really true and how many people are stigmatized because of sensationalized symptoms.

All I do know is that more and more children are being drugged to make it through school. I also know that one of my nephews came to visit when he was ten years old and he came off the plane wired, jerky, and very hyper. He asked me to buy him some coffee and I reacted with an adamant "No way!" But then he explained to me how it would have a calming effect on him, and then, ignoring the stares of other people in the restaurant, I ordered him a coffee and within five minutes he was calm and in control. So having seen that side of things, I do think there is something to this diagnosis but just don't want to see people pushed into if there is something else that can be done.

Doctors do not know everything. They are still seeking resolutions to problems you may not have or that are not the right medications for you. I grew up thinking it wrong to question the authority of doctors, but now I question every pill they give me and I look for natural solutions whenever possible.

Sweet Revenge

When I was younger, I sometimes was not a nice person. This is an example of one of those times. I am not proud of it now, but at the time, I admit I took a great deal of pleasure over the weekend that it occurred.

I lived in a condo in San Francisco in the early eighties. I worked days and was a fairly quiet neighbor. I think I was in my mid-twenties at the time, working as a software developer and I needed to get up around 5:30 am for work. In the unit below me, lived an Italian male, late twenties, who worked some kind of assembly line job on the night shift, from six pm to three am or something like that. All I know is that he would get home from work sometime between three and four am.

I can't recall his name, so we'll call him Steve. Steve liked loud rock and roll. Steve liked to play it loud when he got home at three am.

The first time it happened, I'd lived in the condo for about a month. My bedroom was above my garage so the downstairs unit was beneath my living room. Yet Steve played his music so loud that the bedroom floor vibrated and that's what woke me up.

I called the police. My neighbors called the police. Steve was told to turn it down, to give me his phone number in case of future problems, and everything was fine for another few weeks.

Over and over again he insisted on playing his music loudly when he would get home from work. It didn't happen all the time, but it did continue to happen. The police were called many times, the neighbors around me complained everywhere they could, and nothing changed. He owned his unit and felt that he didn't have to turn the music down if he didn't want to.

Then Steve fell in love. Staci was in her early twenties. She didn't live with Steve but she was often over at his house, even when Steve was at work. So now, instead of occasional loud music in the early am, the music was loud every night when I came home from work.

They got engaged soon after, and I went crazy slowly. Here's where the story gets twisted.

A three day weekend was coming up. I think it was the 4th of July. The idea of having to listen to bass in my apartment the entire weekend was too much to bear. I called the utility companies and had his electric and cable turned off the Friday night at the beginning of the long weekend. I used her name when I was asked who I was.

Steve was very unhappy with Staci. He believed that she had turned off his utilities. So he kicked her to the curb and the condo was quiet for the entire weekend. As a bonus, it took him another week to make up with the girlfriend and to get suspicious as to what happened. He never was sure who it was who actually called the utility companies, but he was a lot better about the music volume for quite a while after that happened.

Of course the quiet didn't last and I eventually moved away. I wasn't a condo owner and so I wasn't stuck living there like he was. I understand that a really large, heavy-footed man rented the unit above him. I am sure they had a joyous time getting along.

While I was really pleased with myself at the time, I am more mature and I don't endorse revenge like this. I learned to live in a house and to avoid noisy neighbors. I pay for the privilege of not having to deal with situations like this. I like living in older neighborhoods where the people are less likely to turn up the stereo on a regular basis. My biggest fear is that someday I will have to live in a condo or apartment again and my neighbor will be a deaf, senior citizen Dead Head or something equally awful. I dread the day when that will happen.

Stuff Can Make You Crazy

I heard about a man today who walked the length of the Amazon River. It took him 2 ½ years. I wondered what he thought about for all that time. I imagine his sense of isolation and wonder if he'd thought to move rocks around in an attempt to clean up the Amazon.

Imagine being alone with your thoughts for that length of time. Would you be able to see clearly at the end of that journey what you should do next? Or would it have been a two year exercise in being stuck at a certain thought and never getting past it. You couldn't talk to anyone about it on an excursion like that.

I imagine that I would think these things while strolling through the Amazon. These are survival thoughts:

When can I stop for a bath?

Is it time for bed yet?

What will I sleep on?

What's for breakfast?

I hope I'm not for breakfast.

Adventures with Ambien and Other Stories

Then, once I ran through all the thoughts concerning my comfort, health, and safety, I'd start wondering about what I would see on my trip.

Will the snakes kill me?

Do they have bugs that crawl in your ears?

What is next on this journey?

What's the history of this place about?

I am so sick of my own thoughts...

Eventually, I think I would wonder about what is next? Will I leave the Amazon with my companion?

And what about the stuff I accumulated on my trip? What do I want to keep when I get back and what do I need to clean out? That leaf and the feather I picked up on my trip is no longer of interest. It is just stuff. And stuff is really meaningless if you don't have a place to keep your stuff.

And stuff (possessions) can drive you crazy. You wonder where to put them, if they are safe, and if anyone else wants them. Remember the movie, *The Gods Must Be Crazy*, where the coca cola bottle fell from the sky and a Kalahari Desert Bushman found it? Remember all the trouble that it caused with his tribe so he tried to find the end of the earth to throw it off of and ends up getting into a lot of trouble.

Decision time: I don't think I will be taking any trips to the Amazon any time soon and I need to get rid of a lot of my stuff. It's keeping me down.

Urban Rules of Etiquette

Call me out: (vb or n) To mock or insult someone or to issue a challenge for them to fight.

When I was growing up (granted, this was in ancient times), my mother used to say *sticks and stones will break my bones, but names will never hurt me.* The purpose of this idiom was to make me tough and to teach me to walk away when people said bad things to me or about me. I was only in one fight during my childhood because I believed turning the other cheek was the right way to act. On the other hand, I was pretty pissed off a lot and ate many things to stuff my feelings, so while I agree in concept with the teaching point, I also think you need to show children how to deal with the anger they feel when they do this. It is no accident that we have a lot of overweight children in the world now. Maybe it should be something like *sticks and stones will break my bones but repressed anger will slowly kill me.*

Imagine a world where we are taught that if someone calls us a name, talks about us behind our back, gossips about us, etc., it is OK to jump them and mess them up.

Adventures with Ambien and Other Stories

Let's take a step forward into a future where that way of behaving is OK in all books. Imagine now, you are in a room with your boss and he is reviewing your last six months of work and he says something less than positive. Let's look into my copy of Urban Rules of Etiquette. Flip, flip, yes, it says here that it is OK to knock that sucker out, give him a little box cutter reminder of this moment, and generally beat him to a pulp.

I see from watching a lot of legal television; shows like Judge Judy or People's Court, in which the parents seem to promote this type of behavior in their children.

Parents say things like "Don't let them insult you or you aren't a man/woman."

It seems to have some kind of machismo or alpha dog root to this type of behavior. In my mind, by encouraging our children to fight when they are picked on like that we are helping to create a world where it is OK to beat up anyone you don't like or who doesn't like you. But that doesn't scale. We can't possibly beat up everyone in the world who disagrees with us or dislikes our point of view. It would be exhausting to even try to defend yourself against the world.

I wouldn't want to be in high school today. I think kids have a much rougher time than I did and I had some pretty miserable moments along the way. But at the end of the day, we need to learn to toughen up and turn our backs on those who are not our fans. Or, forget world peace. We won't even have peace in our own homes.

Bullies

There has been a lot of material around about internet bullying, suicides by people who can't take it, and the type of people who bully others. I thought it was about teenagers acting badly and not people my age. But bullying does not end once we're off the playground; bullies come in all ages.

Bullying is everywhere in the world we live, and we are crying out for change in our schools. We need to cry out for changes in our own backyard. But bullying behavior can be subtle.

I have a friend who loves me, bless her heart. However, if I don't want to do the things she wants to do, she does the following:

- Yells at me, sometimes in a kidding way or sometimes in exasperation.
- Says things like I am being judgmental because she knows I don't like to think I am.
- Says negative things about me and makes me feel like a party pooper or I am too uptight.
- Physically gets close to me so she is in my face.

Adventures with Ambien and Other Stories

Why would I want to be friends with her? For one thing, she is a lot of fun to be with and I like her. For another thing, she doesn't do it in such an obvious way that I was able to label it as bullying behavior, so it has taken me a long time to recognize it. But if you look at the definition, she is bullying me.

I am extremely stubborn and this type of behavior doesn't work well with me. I've seen other people do much worse and I am not friends with people like that. But this woman has enough good qualities that I overlook a little bit of her behavior. I do think if I accused her of doing it she'd be shocked.

So I wonder, if I accept her behavior, am I condoning bullying? Am I endorsing, on some level, the behavior of the kids who caused the death of a teenager? Or what about the kid whose roommate broadcast two sexual episodes he had with another male? He also committed suicide.

I think as a collective society, we are responsible for causing this kind of behavior to occur. Bullies thrive on fear and we are fearful of being wrong, politically incorrect, or of getting involved.

When I was a teenager, two events happened to me:

1. When I was in high school a group of girls tried to intimidate me into giving up a diamond ring I had. They met me en mass in a tunnel under our

school. These were tough girls that were known to fight for what they wanted and I was terrified. They told me, "We want the ring, bitch."

2. I was walking home from work around 11 pm in downtown San Jose and 6 cars of men surrounded me as I cut through a parking lot. They started talking about raping me and I was also scared beyond all reason that night.

In both cases I stood up to the people involved. In the first instance, I just kept walking and said "I don't think so." I had my back to the girls by this time and I just kept going. No one touched me. I lived and I went hmmm.

In the second case, I said, "No way." I took off walking, passing between a couple of the cars and headed east towards my house. I just knew that someone was going to get out of a car and grab me, but no one did. Each car drove slowly by me, the men slung out crass insults, but no one touched me.

Later in life, I ran into one of the girls who confronted me that day and we got to talking. I asked her why she tried to bully me into giving her my jewelry.

She said, "Because it works most of the time, and I get to keep the jewelry. We scare people. But we don't want to fight them for it so if someone stands up to us, we let them go by. You would be surprised at how often it works."

Every time I've stood up to someone, I was terrified. I was sure I was going to be raped, stabbed, or harmed in some way but I did it anyhow. In my thinking, if I am going down, I am doing it with my self-respect intact. I guess that is what is missing in our daily contact with bullies.

Character Flaws

When I was growing up, I always wanted to grow my hair long. My mother thought my hair was too thin and insisted on cutting it short. I think I was twelve before I was allowed to grow it out. When I asked my mother why she'd never let me grow it out, she said that she'd been told that if she kept cutting it, it might grow out thicker. This seemed like crazy thinking to me then and it still does today.

I always wanted to try hair extensions. I'd seen them on others and they looked fabulous. So about five years ago, I bought some and had them put into my hair. They glued them in and it made my hair longer, which was great. One day I went to work with short hair and the next day I had long hair. No one ever asked about it. They did nothing for the overall volume of my hair so eventually I took them out and went back to my shorter, thin look.

I've tried potions and medicines, poultices, and massages. All to no avail. About the only thing that works at all is biotin, which makes your hair grow out thicker and shinier and also makes your nails grow hard. But, you have to patiently take it for months before seeing much of a change.

Today, I wear my hair longer and it is still thin. However, I take biotin to help with the problem.

My mother was a sucker for old wives tales. I am a sucker for modern medicine. If there were magic pills for thick hair or weight loss that were safe, I'd be first in line. I always want to fix something on myself. It's a character flaw...

Watermelon Seeds

My mother always told me not to eat watermelon seeds because they would cause me to grow a watermelon in my belly. The white ones were OK to swallow, but I should not swallow the black ones. Even at seven, this warning never made any sense to me, however I did try to pick out the black seeds whenever I'd get a piece of watermelon.

Once, while trying to eat a watermelon with a fork so I could pick out the seeds, I accidently swallowed some of them. I was frightened that not only would I have this huge watermelon in my belly, but that my mom would think I disobeyed her.

Each day, after brushing my teeth, I would climb up on the sink and open my mouth. Looking into the mirror, I'd have to catch the light just right to see into my throat. I was looking for green leaves indicating that the vine of the watermelon was growing out of it to seek sun. I'd press my fingers into my stomach to see if it was getting harder. I just knew I would be sprouting soon.

My mother caught me looking in my mouth one day and asked me what I was doing. I can still hear her laughing.

Watermelon Seeds Revisited

My stepfather and I were having a conversation once about what my early beliefs in watermelon folklore were about and he told me that he'd always believed that watermelons grew in water. He was about 35 at the time of this conversation.

Watermelon is a fruit with a lot of mythology associated with it. And kids aren't the only gullible ones around. I'm not sure whether he believed it or not, but I think I knew I loved my stepfather when we had that moment and I believed that he believed in things that didn't make any sense. I wasn't the only gullible person in the world.

If Life is a Highway…

On the way home from work today, a young man (looking like he was in the Military) drove up quickly behind me with his lights on. I was going 65 and while I wanted to get home, I wasn't in any huge hurry—at least not like he appeared to be. I tapped my brakes to let him know to back off. I was in the slow lane. Eventually he pulled over when the lanes opened up to an off ramp and proceeded to follow less than one car length behind someone else. I was dismayed that someone would follow so closely on the freeway, but I also wondered what he had ahead of him that made him in such a hurry.

I'm not sure if this satisfaction with my life that I'd only begun to experience in the last few years was what had helped me slow into a normal driver. I don't know if it had anything to do with my attitude, as I was always quite a speeder when I was younger. But at the age of 50-something, I was content to drive a little more sedately and I wouldn't think to follow that closely behind another car.

I actually drive a sports car and people have asked me how I could afford the insurance. I always flippantly replied that I drove like an old lady. Well, I do. I drive like a lady with someplace to go who wants to enjoy the drive along the way. Whatever is at the end of the drive will be there whether I get there in ten minutes or thirty. And I used to notice when I was younger and driving faster, that for all that speed, the slower drivers usually ended up right behind me. I risked tickets and accidents only to end up in the same place as the calm, stress free driver.

The man in the car drove on. I never saw him again, but I wondered if he made a real difference by arriving a minute sooner, by putting other people's lives at risk, and by risking his own life and limb. What was waiting for him at the other end that caused him to drive so recklessly?

Perception

It amazes me at the differences between how I see myself and my potential when I compare it to what other people see. I had to do an exercise for a class once. I don't remember all the questions I was supposed to ask five people who worked with me but I remember some of them. Try this yourself and see if your results are what you wanted/expected or if something else comes up out of the conversation.

1. What do you see as my strength?
2. What do you see as my weakness?
3. Is there anything you'd like to say to me that you felt you weren't able to say?
4. Is there anything you would like to know about me?
5. Is there anything I would like you to know about me?
6. What does everybody know about me?
7. What can you count on me for?
8. What can you never count on me for?

9. Is there anything you want to be acknowledged for by me that I haven't acknowledged?
10. What is it like to be my manager?
11. What do I bring to the table?
12. What do you find annoying about being my manager?
13. What behavior(s) would you suggest I alter?
14. What do you see as my attributes?
15. What do you see as my weaknesses?

When I started asking people I knew some of these questions, their answers surprised me. The things they saw as important enough to mention were things I didn't consider important (until they mentioned it), or I was surprised to be seen a particular way in their view. For instance, at work I was thought to be demanding, when all I'd ever asked for was the knowledge and tools to support the work I did so I wouldn't have to bother anyone else. That was a very shocking revelation. I actually learned that just because I do my job alone and without other people, what I did impacted other people, put demands on their time that I had no visibility into, and in short, caused other people to do work that I didn't know about.

How would you like to learn that about yourself when you thought you were just doing your job and that when you were done, the job was complete? I think it was very naive of me not to see that my work would impact others like that but that was something I only learned by asking those questions.

I thought I was pretty aware of what people thought and said about me until I did this exercise, when I found out that I knew nothing really. It's like the more you learn the less you know...

Calling on People

I have always been able to pick up the phone and talk to strangers. I actually sold light bulbs by phone while earning money for college. I can talk to anyone on the phone and was the top sales person consistently while I worked that job.

Talking face-to-face with people used to be more of a problem. Their proximity would make me very nervous. But then I took a course where one of the exercises is to stand nose-to-nose with someone else for what seemed like a very long time. At the end of the exercise, you realize that looking at people, being in their presence, only means what you want it to. In my case, it meant nothing except to give me peace to feel comfortable in the presence of strangers. What a breakthrough!

We are all just five year old children walking around in grownup bodies. We all have the same fears and hopes and we all feel we are not worthy in some way and so we mask it. But at the end of the day, it

Lin Laurie

is that inner child that has the most effect on how we are as adults.

Being Invisible

In my teens, I was a pretty young woman with the world at my feet. People tried to talk to me and they were interested in me, I thought. Hah, I was naïve and green as a country boy visiting the big city for the first time. Now I am in my 50's and have crow's feet and wrinkles. When I was 19, my character was undeveloped, my education was unformed, and I only thought of myself in terms of how men saw me. I related to everyone flirtatiously, as if that were the only thing about me I knew to put out there.

I am so thankful that the past is far back in my life. I know I have character and grace, have a voice that people listen to, and a writing that attracts fans. I know I do good work, am a giving, loving person, and I have learned and loved a lot. Plus, I'm still pretty cute and know how to flirt like an expert. There is so much freedom in those realizations.

Some of my friends have mentioned this thing that happens with men and younger people as they age. It seems to start around forty for most women, but that's not necessarily true. It can happen at any age. It is a sense of invisibleness: they feel invisible; people look through them, call on others in line, or walk by them without eye contact. I experienced it one time and I knew that at the time it happened to me I was feeling extremely low and depressed, and my self-esteem was in the toilet. I am absolutely sure that I contributed to that experience by sending out this energy with the message "don't look at me. I don't want you to see how I feel today". I didn't like the experience at all and since then I've held my head high, looked people right in the eyes as if to say "You cannot negate or disappear me." So far it seems to be working.

When I walk down the corridors at work, head held high and meet people's eyes, it's funny but they say hello. Or sometimes I do it first just to play with people's energy. But if I walk down the same halls with my head hung low and refuse to meet people's eyes, it is like being invisible. Try it yourself and see how it works. Say hello to people in the halls as you pass and watch what happens.

At work, people also tend to talk to me in lines or when I'm in the kitchen waiting for my tea to get hot. People connect when the energy they want to connect with is there. Like magnets, energy pulls others with the same energy towards itself. So now I always hold my head up high, make eye contact, and avoid that invisible feeling.

Human beings are energy and that energy can be felt by the people around us. If we want to be liked, we have to like ourselves enough to feel like we are worthy of being liked by others. You start by standing tall and looking the world in the eye. I urge you to play with your experiences and see what happens to your life and your feelings about yourself.

Secrets and Lies

A friend of mine once said that if you had a secret you should either shout it from the roof tops or crush in between the ground your feet so that people won't know. So unless you are the only one that knows a secret, cop to it and own it so it doesn't own you.

I have very few secrets and with each one that I give away, I notice a feeling of lightness that comes over me. I still have a few left, but I now have the confidence to know that because of time and distance, they don't own me. I am not my secrets and they are not me. And those who know about them love me anyway, so while I still hold back on a couple of things, I've never lost a friend by telling them the worst about me. A friend has never lost me either by telling me something they held close to their heart. If you get to the point where you can have that kind of conversation, then you must already be pretty good friends who can judge character and so whatever it is shouldn't matter.

I've talked about this with several friends. The little kid inside of us can't accept that we are good or worthy or lovable. We are harder on ourselves that others usually are. We are the last to forgive ourselves when we do something wrong and the first to beat ourselves up over it. But our secrets are only at their worst when they are sealed away and we hide that part of who we are from the people we love in our life. I'm only now getting to the point in life where I can forgive the five year old judgmental brat that lives inside and show that brat to those I love without fear of being disliked.

When it comes to lying, I've noticed that if you don't tell lies, you don't have to recall what you said. It's much easier to sleep at night when you aren't trying to figure out whether or not you told someone something that wasn't quite the way it happened. When you're young, I think you have a little more mental energy and can juggle the lies more easily than you can when you get older. I can't say I don't tell someone they look wonderful when they don't, but I try to keep my integrity intact and try to phrase anything I say as the truth.

Affairs of the Heart

I was married only briefly in the late eighties, and I was more responsible for the breakup than my husband. I used to be comforted by that fact, but really it didn't matter who was responsible. When you take vows in front of God and then say "oops, I made a mistake. I want a redo," the hurt is felt on both sides and everyone has some blame.

I am only now, after twenty years of single life, coming to terms with the issues that I held onto after my divorce. I felt like such a failure and was afraid to risk the pain of being in love with someone else for all those years. Even the man I've been seeing on and off for the last eight years has never heard me say, "I love you." I adore him, I am very attached to him, but I can't say more. I think saying the words makes me more vulnerable to being hurt.

I am actually not sure if I do love him. I desire him. I am entertained by him. I care about what he thinks and feels. I like to make him happy and I want to be in his company. I am missing that overwhelming feeling I associate with love. Both times I've been in love when I was younger, there came a time when I was just blown over by the awareness of being in love and wanting someone enough to not care about the consequences. I don't quite feel that way about this man.

Before I got married, I made my future husband go in with me for Aids testing. We went into the clinic and gave blood and then we waited a week or so for the test results to come back. When we went into the clinic to find out the results, we were called into different rooms at the same time. I went in one room to speak with a nurse and was back out in the waiting room in less than five minutes.

I waited.

And I waited some more.

And again, I waited. By now I was sure he had Aids and then in the next moment I knew that I loved him and would stay with him no matter what the diagnosis was.

Still, I continued to wait.

After about thirty minutes, the door opened to the room he was in, and I could hear laughter. He'd been sitting in the room all that time telling jokes.

I was mad, I was relieved, and I knew then that I was in love with him and when he asked me to marry him later that month, I was happy to say yes.

Hogzilla!

I spent a few hours sick in a hotel room recently while attending a conference. I ended up moaning in pain from a badly upset stomach and eating an entire roll of Tums while watching three hours of Hogs Gone Wild on the Discovery Channel. Apparently the world is being overrun by fat, ugly, feral hogs, and boars. They have become a problem in 40 U.S. states as well as in Europe, and can weigh as much as 1200 pounds. Holy Batman! That's a lot of nasty pork.

This was news to me! I got online to investigate.

They came to America in 1539 by Hernando De Soto or Christopher Columbus, depending on who you agree with. They interbred with Russian wild boars to become larger and more dangerous, and this interbreeding or hybrid hog is greatly contributing to the wild hog problem. They are aggressive, live 6-8 years, and the sows can breed approximately 1000 swine in their lifetime.

The hogs are encroaching on civilization, eating small pets, rooting around in yards, and causing a great deal of property damage. In addition, they carry some nasty diseases.

Hog hunts attract hunters from all over. In Texas, you can get a two-for-one hog hunting package. But hunters can't keep up with the breeding habits of these nasty beasts. In San Diego, they recently allowed hunters to bag two hogs each, although the season was relatively short.

Here's what one hog hunting package contained (sic):

The ranch hand hog hunt package can be used year-round with no closed seasons!

Adventures with Ambien and Other Stories

This is a 3 day, 2 night wild hog hunt package, and includes:

- 1 hog of any size; no trophy fees
- Any 2 predators or varmints per day (Bobcat, Coyote, Fox, Possum, Armadillo, Raccoon, Rabbit, Ringtail Cat, or Mountain lion. We only see a few mountain lion per year, but we want them shot on sight!)
- Day & Night hunting sessions
- All Meals and Drinks
- Great Lodging
- Full Ranch Staff

Not included:

- Hunting license ($48 non-resident Adult, $7 for under 17 yrs old) @ Walmart)
- Hog Cleaning (up to 100 lbs. is $35.00 to gut, skin, and quarter. Add $10 per 50 lbs thereafter. Example, a 200 lb hog would be $55.
- Taxidermy prep to cape $20
- Gratuity for your staff

We have to kill those varmints! I am not a fan of hunting but was fascinated by the number of opportunities that exist out there to let your inner killer come out to play.

Lin Laurie

The hunting aspect of hog hunting is really fascinating. They use "work" dogs to run down and trap a wild boar. These dogs are trained specifically to hunt hogs and are usually pit bulls or other aggressive breeds. They wear protection and other items consisting of GPS devices, neck collars that protect their necks, covers that protect their organs and mid-section, and lights that both illuminate the way and help the hunters find and follow the dogs.

The hunters can attend competitions and other events to both bond and challenge with other hunters. Hunters are predominately male, but the occasional female does find her way into the hunt.

When I returned home after the conference, I will confess to programming my DVR to record additional episodes. I can't tell you exactly what aspect of this weird sport fascinated me, but for some reason I felt compelled to view shows like Hogs Gone Wild and Hogzilla.

Hogzilla, a purported 1000-pound feral hog the size of a pick-up truck, is a monster pig from South Georgia, and will soon be made into a horror movie. Gonzo hog attacks small village type of thing; use your imagination for what I am sure will be captivating viewing.

I guess what I find so amazing is that there is a whole world of people out there whose focus is to do something I never even thought about but they take for granted. Like being worried that an alligator would grab your pet. This is outside of my reality so completely. San Diego has no alligators or hogs as far as I know. But we do have coyotes who steal our small pets in the night. I could really get behind a show on coyote trapping since that is a danger in my world.

One night, when it is late and very quiet, if you hear a low rumbled rutting in your yard, get out your dog and a shot gun. Son of Hogzilla might be coming to visit you and steal your small children.

Why Do People Do This?

At a recent software conference I was standing around just people watching and a woman came up to me to complain. She didn't get her wakeup call... The hotel should have a backup alarm system... Now she was missing breakfast... I don't know why she thought I'd be receptive to her complaints or would be able to do anything about them. I may as well have been a fly on the wall for all the good her complaints did her by telling them to me.

Breakfast was still being served, not ten feet from where we stood, yet she preferred to continue talking to someone who couldn't help her instead of cutting her losses and grabbing a bite. A hotel staff member happened to walk by and I passed her off on the poor unsuspecting but good humored woman and I walked away. A little later, I walked downstairs and saw the same woman talking to someone I knew so I walked over. The woman (who was wearing a band aid above her right eye and was very memorable), was now complaining to the conference staff about how she'd now missed breakfast and was now missing the first class in her conference series. As far as I could tell, she'd complained to absolutely no one who could help her, yet she continued to look for more people to talk to.

Many years ago, a therapist told me a story about a woman who wanted an avocado so she went to the grocery store. She walks back to the vegetable section and looks around. She doesn't see any avocados for sale and she is angry. After all, she is a grocery store and that is where avocados should be found. It is her right to have an avocado when she wants one!

She finds the clerk who stocks the fruits and vegetables and asks him where the avocados are located.

He says, "I'm sorry but avocados are out of season so we don't have any in stock right now."

"But that's not fair. I want an avocado. Where's the manager? I want to complain about your lack of avocados. He should be able to find me an avocado! What kind of grocery store is this anyway?"

So the clerk helps her locate the manager and she asks the manager for an avocado.

"I'm sorry ma'am, we are out of avocados. They are not in season right now. But we have some great guacamole in aisle five. Let me help you find it."

"This is not right. You are not a good grocery store. I want an avocado right now."

Well, the moral of the story is that you can't always get what you want, but you can control what you ask for and make what you need happen. And if your family is like the grocery store and has no love for you because it is out of season or it doesn't meet your expectations, you can choose to go to another store (or family or lover) to get what you need or form your own little life coop. I got that message pretty early in life and was able to create a life with wonderful friends who give me the love and respect I didn't feel I got from my family.

But it's funny how the things I thought I wanted when I was younger, I now realize I had; they just didn't come in a recognized package. My family isn't the Ozzie and Harriet kind of family I'd wanted. Sometimes the people in my life didn't always do what I wanted or expected but it didn't mean they didn't love me. In any case, I stopped beating my head against a door that couldn't open and I stopped bugging people about an avocado when they had none to give me. I hope band aide woman figures this out and spends her next conference focused on the opportunities instead of dwelling on the problems. I am sure she will have a much better time if she does that both in future conferences as well as in life.

Walk Softly and Don't Use the Phone

Sometimes I do personal development work and have the opportunity to observe other people in the midst of dealing with personal pain. A person, who stood out in a class full of conflicted individuals was involved in a field of work that required her to make a great deal of phone calls and she was terrified. She didn't know when the best time to call would be; she didn't know what to say to solicit clients; she didn't want to bother anyone and so of course it was crippling her and depressing her.

In addition, when I asked her what her husband thought about her problem, she said she couldn't ask him... She didn't want to bother her husband. I was completely shocked. Wow, what a checked out marriage that must have been if she couldn't trust her mate with a simple question.

I am the opposite. I can call Obama or Gandhi (if he were still alive and don't test me). I sold light bulbs

Adventures with Ambien and Other Stories

over the phone in college and was always the top earner. I then up sold vitamins, increasing each sale by another $20-40. It was an odd product pairing, but it worked and helped me get through a year of college. I began using a prepared script and then improvised it to meet my own personality quirks. Most of the customers were older (I was in my early 20's at the time) and some were lonely and enjoyed having someone to talk to. The products were good, so I felt OK with what I was doing.

Would I want to do it now? No. But it was invaluable experience in helping me deal with any sales or phone calling fears. I can cold-call anyone. I have no fear for the phone. Besides, I will never meet these people so if they say no, it isn't a personal thing so I don't take it as rejection against me. I wish I could give some of my knowledge and fearlessness to the woman with the problem. But having a script is the best thing to do to help fearful people get into action and start calling.

Calling on strangers in person is much more demanding because you are showing up in someone's office, warts and all. But I seem to do fine with it so that's helped me gain confidence over the years. I had a mentor when I was in my twenties who told me once that if you don't know how to do something, pretend you do (you can draw on prior experience or a TV show) and eventually you will know how to do it. That simple advice has helped me in so many ways to push my own personal limitations.

I've also been a skip tracer for a rental furniture company and had to pretend I was a neighbor or sister to get the information that would help my company either get paid or get our furniture back. People would rent that furniture and skip out for places unknown. I would find them, even when they went to Saudi Arabia or Alaska. I had a great track record of success in getting back the furniture or the money. And we didn't have the web to use. I'm sure I could do that job much better and much faster today.

Anyhow, these were great experiences for me in terms of bolstering self-esteem and confidence. I am always looking for opportunities that let me push my own personal boundaries. I've always been the kind of person who challenges anything that constrains me.

The phone phobia woman came back to our class a week later and had made some significant small improvements. She was starting to call people for her business who had asked her to call and she was finding acceptance and need for her services. The ironic part was that these people had asked her to call them but she just got caught up in her own fear and confusion and was absolutely stopped. Her success both shocked her and made her feel better.

The nice thing about doing personal development work is when you see it working and you see the gratitude of the person who a week earlier was struggling so hard and having such a bad time. After struggling to find a way to make their new knowledge fit and work in their lives, they come back and their faces light up, they smile, they raise their eyes to look at you, and they are happy with each small improvement.

As I get older I am doing more of this work because it makes me feel much more comfortable with myself and it gives me a process for working through my own issues. One thing I know now is that we never get rid of our issues, but we are able to learn ways to deal with them so they no longer stop us. That's the path to leading an unstoppable life full of inspiration, love, abundance, and joy. That's what I aspire to and that's why I continue to do personal development work. I want to contribute to my family and my friends and even complete strangers in a way that leaves them touched, moved, and inspired by me and by the possibilities that they are.

In Between the Lines

As a child, I remember spending many hours perfecting my ability to draw without going outside the lines. Intellectually, I know I was learning muscle control in my hands so I could be more exact in my coloring, but I didn't really think much about the other lessons to be had in a coloring book.

As an adult, one day while driving down the road it came to me that coloring books were a method of teaching us something much deeper and darker. Stay inside the lines; don't violate the rules; do what is expected, don't use crazy colors...

Some of these are good lessons. After all, we can't have an orderly world if everyone drives on whatever side of the road they feel like taking. We can't have creative driving if we want to survive the experience. If we don't obey the laws of our society then we'd have a world of chaos and confusion. On the other hand, we've built a world that is in some ways over legislated, where everyone shows their politically correct face in public. When are the lines too much? Sometimes the principal of the thing is too confining when put into practice. I wonder where this will lead us.

Children first start scribbling in a coloring book. There is no form to their art; they just take the crayon anywhere they want. Sometimes they push it outside of the picture, across the table, and it ends up being dropped on the floor. Then over time, they start to tighten up on that crayon and soon they are coloring inside the lines, creating shades of color, and maturing in their use of the coloring book.

It is the same with a child's spirit. When we are born, we have no limits, no politically correct rules to abide by, and no restrictions. We don't know a hurt feeling from a toy truck. Then slowly, we learn society's rules, and slowly our spirit is boxed in and the spirit dulls. Children are inquisitive, adventurous, and open spirits. Are you? Am I? It's all that stuff that we add to our day—all the meaning we give things over the years that deadens our spirit and can make us feel hopeless.

I want to get some of that spirit back. I want to believe each day is new and exciting and a great adventure. I want to see possibility instead of probability when I wake up in the morning. In writing this book I can try. I want to run through my life arms held high, screaming ahhhhh as she runs towards life.

No, I can do it. If you come to San Diego and you see some crazy looking red head dancing in the waves during an early, lazy summer morning, say hello. It will be me. Unless it's you...

Contact List Mania

I have a huge contact list that has come about by doing years of networking, working with people as a contractor all over the country, and being fastidious

Lin Laurie

about entering names into the list. But this list wasn't giving me much personal power. It felt like this list of people who were no longer in my life, some of whom I'd experienced difficulties with, and all in all, something I didn't really like looking at or scrolling through.

Recently, after taking a powerful course called Communication – Access to Power, I came to see that contact list in a different light. Each name was someone I could call and talk to. I could ask them for something or just talk about nothing. These were people I knew and who knew me. I could ask for what I wanted from any of these people. They didn't have to give it to me but there was nothing stopping me from asking for what I wanted except my own mind. This realization opened huge doors to expanding my networking opportunities. My contacts may not all like me but they did know me so that was one foot in the door. And whether people liked me or not, everyone liked the work I did. Besides, if they would say no, then it was just no. It didn't destroy my world, leave me humiliated and ashamed or in any way negatively harm me. It was just a conversation with an answer at the end. It meant nothing more.

I had a problem around this time with my niece. She lived in Minneapolis and I didn't see her much. But she'd spent the first two years of her life living with me and her mom, and we were very close. She'd fly out twice a year throughout her childhood to visit me and we had a wonderful relationship. But she'd announced she was pregnant with her second baby on Facebook, instead of telling me the news with a phone call. I was incredibly hurt and I realized that I really had a problem with my niece.

The problem was that she was having a second child without any way of supporting it. She and the father were not working and he was a former gang member. I really disapproved and was scared for my niece. And, I felt that since I'd been a surrogate parent to her, I'd failed in passing down my values to her. So I really felt like I was being totally rejected. I was judging, she was mad, and she shut me down.

Since I was taking this communication class, I decided to use the situation with my niece as an exercise for the class.

We were told to listen in a way we never had before:

- To listen to the other party and do not spend the listening time thinking about the next thing you will say. Just be there and be present to the conversation. What a concept—to actually listen!
- Acknowledge something or say something positive about the other person. This is such a powerful tip.

Lin Laurie

- Be willing and ready to give up your old way of thinking or being. In other words, give up negative talk or any agenda that you might have for the call.

So I placed a call to my niece and I told her I loved her and I just asked her how she was. I asked about her daughter and I asked about her boyfriend, just to make sure they were all OK. I told her how much I loved her and how important my relationship with her was.

I told her I'd been thinking about when she was about two years old and how I was taking us swimming that day. I remembered how full of life she was, all happy, and squirming in her seat like little kids do. I was happy to be in the car with her and happy in the moment. So I made up a silly little song about us being wild women, swimmin' women, whooo hooo. Silly little song that didn't rhyme or anything. We sang it out, we laughed, and we had a wonderful time that day. I told her what a special memory that was for me.

"It's funny, Aunt Linda, that you would mention that memory. I just took my daughter swimming for the first time this week and I was singing that song to her."

In that moment, I realized that not only had I had an effect on her life, but that by passing it down to her

Adventures with Ambien and Other Stories

daughter, that moment lived on, and would live on, long after I was dead. She'd given me a legacy.

Wow. And it gets even better.

The next day, my niece sent me this note:

Hey,

Yes i love you very much and you are a big part in my life and i always enjoy talking to you. I was wondering if you had a web cam. If so we could talk kind of in person and you could really see your great niece. I would really like you to be a part of her life the same way you have always been a part of mine. Even though growing up is hard and i don't get to visit as much as i would like to that would be a great way to connect for us. Well i love you let me know if u do and i will direct you on how we could do this.

Now you have to know that I have been a technical writer and trainer of computer software for over 30 years and my niece wanted to give me instructions on how to do webcam so she can include me more in her life. And I let her! In her next email she wrote her own instructions for downloading a Google application and setting it up. I was so proud!

Communication is a wonderful, powerful tool and anyone who can do that well can rule the world. I am proud to be working on my abilities, improving my relationships with family and friends, and in taking those skills back to my workplace.

Today, I don't look down at the ground when I walk by someone. Instead, I say hello and look them in the eye if they look up. Just doing that has made a huge difference in my workplace. I play with it. When I start a new contract, I notice people who aren't looking me in the eye and make a game to see how long before I can get them to initiate a hello to me.

Sometimes you see something from another point of view and it helps to change the way you communicate. Another homework assignment in this course was to try to see something from another point of view. In looking at my niece, and that situation, I realized that by judging and disapproving, I gave her no good place to be at when we talked. She could only defend her choices instead of sharing the joy of her child with me. By giving up the judging, I could see other ways to talk to her. I didn't have to like her boyfriend, but I didn't have to disparage him either. Once I started doing that, she stopped coming from a defensive position and our relationship has vastly improved. Today I use my webcam to unite us and to include ourselves in each other's lives. She's still pregnant and still with the same guy, but she no longer puts the distance of Facebook between us when she has important news to share.

Adventures with Ambien and Other Stories

Perspective is a funny thing. We all have our own way of looking at a situation. But in making my house cat safe for a new pet I brought home, I needed to get down on my hands and knees and look at my house from the cat's perspective. I came to realize that things look a lot different at my house when you are looking at life through a cat's eyes compared to what I saw from my 5'4" view. And in doing that physically, I came to realize that it could be done mentally as well. And that is why you have your story of why your brother stole your doll when you were five, and your brother has his side where he only took it because you broke his prized truck. You didn't see or remember that part of the story but both points of view can be right, you can both tell the same story and have very different feelings about it, and you can both get over whatever it is that has you stuck in your relationship.

Sometimes I part my hair on the opposite side of my head or wear something in a way I usually wouldn't just to shift myself from my comfort zone so I can observe things from another position. It's a silly little game I play but it sometimes helps me see another position when I feel stuck in a particular way of being.

Laurie

Adventures with Ambien

I became an insomniac when I was twenty-eight and my fiancé had committed suicide. I would drop off to sleep just fine, but would wake up at about 1 am and would usually stay awake until about 3 am. I was affected by this disorder intermittently until my early fifties. When it would get bad I'd use PM Tylenol, and it would go away after a few days, but stress aggravated the condition greatly.

In 2008, I was laid off from one of my favorite companies a second time and had two months of notice to serve. That situation was bad enough, but then one of my brothers died. He was about 45 when he died; one of the younger ones. It was sudden and not at all expected—he had a car accident and died about four miles from my parent's house in Northern California. I hadn't spoken to him in a couple of years but had been trying to reach him in the months leading up to his death. Needless to say, both of these experiences drove me to seek out a pharmaceutical approach to sleep, and thus I became an Ambien user.

Ambien is one of a variety of newer sleep medications approved as a short term solution for sleep deprivation. Side effects can include:

- Nausea or vomiting
- Anterograde amnesia

Adventures with Ambien and Other Stories

- Hallucinations, through all physical senses, of varying intensity
- Delusions
- Altered thought patterns
- Ataxia or poor motor coordination, difficulty maintaining balance
- Euphoria and/or dysphoria
- Increased appetite
- Increased Libido or decreased libido / destrudo
- Amnesia
- Impaired judgment and reasoning
- Uninhibited extroversion in social or interpersonal settings
- Increased impulsivity
- When stopped, rebound insomnia may occur
- Headaches in some people
- Short term memory loss

Let's just start with impairing balance. I only found that one out in researching this story. I would have trouble standing on one leg, would get dizzy walking on a curb, and sometimes just had trouble with coordination. I thought it was just a symptom of old age and didn't connect it to the medication for a very long time. That's not so bad if it is a short term problem, but I ended up taking this medication for four years and had a horrible

Lin Laurie

struggle to get off of it. It isn't the medication that is addictive, but the desire to get a good night's sleep.

Once, while looking in the refrigerator, I found a screw driver in the vegetable drawer. Interesting as I didn't recall putting it there, and yet there it was.

Another time, I was going to turn on the oven and I opened the door to make sure there was nothing in it. I sometimes put bread in there when I want to see a clean kitchen. There's not a lot of storage in my kitchen and I sometimes ran out of room. Anyhow, I opened the door and there was a small goose necked lamp. I did remember heading to the garage a few days earlier with the lamp. I guess I got distracted somewhere along the way from my office to the kitchen. I'm not sure how it got in the oven, but I am glad I checked the oven before turning it on.

One Saturday morning, I woke up early with a little voice in my head telling me, "Must go to Home Depot." So I got dressed in a robot-like state, and drove the six blocks to the store. Once inside, I loaded my cart with over $500 worth of home and garden supplies like a hedge trimmer, bags of dirt, and some paint. I had a gardener and I didn't do yard work so I have no idea why I needed the hedge trimmer. I drove home, left my purchases in the car and went back to bed. When I woke up later, I realized what I had done and I returned most of the items to the store. I did keep a couple of things that I'd needed. I don't know if my thinking about it the night before was what caused me to mindlessly shop for tools.

One morning, I woke up to see a beer sitting on my nightstand. I don't drink at home alone so my first thought was that someone had stood there drinking and watching me sleep. I was really frightened. Then I walked into the kitchen and looked in the sink. There were some dishes stacked neatly there and I realized I'd done some sleep eating. I don't think it was an accident that I'd gained 20 lbs. since starting on this medication.

There were many other times I'd gotten up to eat something in the middle of the night. However, this time was different in that I had absolutely no memory of getting up and cooking anything.

Several times I found I'd thrown things away that were brand new. Once in particular, I'd bought some new allergy medication and when I later went looking for it, I found it staring up at me from the garbage can.

Another time, when a friend of mine ended up sleeping over, I woke up at about 3 am and ordered a new Kindle, a cover, and a skin. Everything was all in bright pink. Fortunately, I did want a Kindle and I

Lin Laurie

love the color pink, so it wasn't a problem. However, I have had things delivered to my house that I didn't recall ordering and of course that cost me money. Usually the things I got were things I wanted so my subconscious must have been controlling my buying habits. Yet it was disturbing to think that I did things without a memory of them.

So far I've bought the following items without memory:

- Kindle and accessories
- An umbrella for my patio table
- A wheel for my wheel barrow
- Six large bags of earth
- A hedge trimmer
- A large garbage can
- A hammock stand without a hammock – I later went back and purchased the hammock as it was a pretty cool stand.
- Couch pillows
- A Bose home entertainment system – This was my most expensive purchase and another robotic shopping trip, this time to Fry's. I'd seen it in the store a week earlier and wanted it but I hadn't planned to buy it.

There have been several times that found I'd invited people to parties and other things that I'd been thinking about when I went to sleep, but I have very little conscious idea of sending out invitations. It made life interesting for a while. I ended up checking my Outlook Outbox in the morning to see what I'd done and I configured it so that messages would not go out until I clicked Send a second time. Other times I recall wanting to send someone an email so I would think about it and later find out I'd sent it but I had no memory of writing it.

I am struggling to get off Ambien now. But when I try, I suffer from rebound insomnia. I think it is rebound, but who knows where the original insomnia ends and the rebound begins. To me it all looks like I am unable to sleep.

There is something good to be said for insomnia though. It helped me write this book. My peak writing time was between 1-3 am whenever I couldn't sleep. Many years ago a doctor told me to get out of bed and just do something until I felt sleepy again. So I've written this book, I've written about half of a mystery, I've cleaned house, and I've gotten a lot of dreary office tasks done while I couldn't sleep.

When I first got insomnia, I had three jobs, thinking I may as well use it to my advantage. But I was thirty years younger and I don't have that much energy now. I've tried to keep a good attitude over the many years I've suffered from it. I went back to college while I had it and found plenty of time to do my homework.

The only cures I know for insomnia are to do a lot of exercise during the day and to avoid as much stress as possible. Those activities seem to keep me glued to my bed at night. But if you live on this planet you can't help feeling stressed out from time to time. Other than that, nothing seems to work for me on a consistent basis.

Insomnia is also a health problem. Lack of sleep contributes to:

- Automobile and machinery accidents
- Lowered immune system's ability to fight infections
- Increased sleep walking
- Raised blood pressure
- Hallucinations
- And many other delightful symptoms

I've been so tired at different times that I've had to pinch my hands with my fingernails until they break through the skin while in meetings so I can stay awake. I've gone into restrooms and closed my eyes for ten minutes or so to get some rest. I've drunk so much coffee that my stomach hurts, it gave me an ulcer, and I've come close to falling asleep while driving.

Using Ambien, I don't have to suffer from insomnia, just from the side effects of the medication. Both are bad so it is difficult to have to choose between two lists of such "wonderful" options.

Inspirational Women

Every once in a while I will get asked the question about who did I think were the two most inspirational females that influenced me when I was growing up. I always answer the same, despite having to defend the answer every time.

Lucille Ball – Lucy broke through a lot of ceilings. She played a housewife on I Love Lucy but she pushed against female stereotypes in her show. She always respected Ricky but she wanted power of her own. Growing up in the sixties when women were beginning to struggle for jobs and promotions and financial worth, she was someone who believed in herself, never stopped trying to find her own place in her life, and was still loyal to her family and friends.

But it gets better. Lucille Ball was one of the first women to head a production company. She was also fundamental to the creation and production of I Love Lucy, and used it as a vehicle to try to keep her marriage to Desi Arnaz together. After they split, she purchased his shares of Desilu Productions and later pioneered many methods still used in television production to this day.

While today Lucille Ball's characterization of a zany housewife is dated and women today have greatly exceeded her accomplishments, she was a trail blazer and she contributed hugely to my own aspirations by being the role model she was.

The second woman I attribute as having a huge imprint on my attitudes and interests in life wasn't always a woman, but several writers who authored Nancy Drew mysteries using the pen name, Carolyn Keene.

Nancy Drew was a fictional character created in the 1930's. She was an independent teenage, amateur detective. These books attempted to erase racial and sexual stereotypes and were inspirational to teenaged girls and reproduced in 45 languages.

When I was ten years old, our next door neighbor Tim, had a biking accident and went off the dirt road at the end of our street, down a hill, and crashed into a rock, causing him to pass out, fall over, and almost drown in a stream (we called it Little River). My brother and I got his head out of the water, and then I rode my bike up to the ambulance and fire department at the top of our street. My brother and I saved his life and his sister was so grateful that she gave me a large box of

Nancy Drew mysteries, beginning my long history of longing for a different life I didn't know it until probably 20 years later, but they were first additions and today have some value. I thought my niece would love them one day, so I've held onto them now for forty-five years, but about ten years ago she clued me into the fact that Nancy Drew is old hat and there are many more modern books she could and would be reading. So I've kept them, and now I really don't know what to do with them. I think about putting them on E-Bay, but I am really fond of them and everything they represent.

Other Writings

I have written two other books. The first is a mystery about a serial killer who terrorizes Seattle and kills prostitutes. It's called the Death of Dirty Angels, and I almost got it published using the traditional methods (not self-publishing). I got as far as getting an agent who wanted changes made to the book, and instead of doing the changes, I moved to California and didn't write anything else for more than five years. I developed a huge fear of success that took me eight years to overcome.

This mystery was extremely accurate. I did a lot of research, took a certificate program in mystery and suspense writing, and also took another certificate program in forensics from the University of Washington. I dated a couple of Seattle police

Lin Laurie

officers, and befriended several others, including the detective (Bob Keppel) that Ted Bundy confessed to before being put to death in 1989.

Bob also taught other classes at University of Washington like Introduction to Serial Killers, and Serial Killers 101. He was a very nice and yet fascinating man who wrote several novels, was featured prominently in Ann Rule's book, "The Stranger Beside Me," and was one of the best known detectives in the US if not worldwide.

I was extremely flattered when I did a homework assignment that involved a PowerPoint presentation on Gerald Stanos, a Florida serial killer who was housed with Ted Bundy up until Ted was executed. Bob Keppel asked if he could keep my presentation to use when he gave talks at conferences. He thought I'd done that good of a job on it. Of course I said yes.

I also took classes on the Green River case, where Gary Ridgeway was accused of killing 49 prostitutes, and is suspected of killing many more. I went with a good friend who was also a mystery writer to his arraignment, where many of the victims' parents were present and grieving. Interestingly, my friend (who also shared my interest) and I were suspected by the press covering the event, of being related to victims and we had to run a gauntlet of reporters who wanted to interview us. We ended up being seen running down the corridors of the courthouse on the news that night. I had no idea of the kind of treatment that grieving friends and family were subjected to until that day and it was a shocking eye opener.

One of the amazing things I discovered that day was that serial killers come in all forms and they don't necessarily look like monsters with teeth dripping in blood. Gary Ridgeway was a small, unassuming man who answered "not guilty" in a soft-spoken voice when the judge read off each count of murder. Had I met him on the streets I'd never have expected that he was a violent man. But I've been told that this is exactly why serial killers like him and Ted Bundy were so successful. They were so normal looking and acting until they had women in their control. Then no more Mr. Nice Guy, hello axe, knife, gun, etc.

In my forensics program, we had many people come in as guest lecturers, including one of Gary's two lawyers. I also went to school with one of his jailers and I got a lot of insight by talking about how he was behaving in jail. I also attended lectures by the medical examiner that autopsied Kurt Cobain (Nirvana lead singer) and Lance Staley (Alice in Chains lead singer). The classes were fascinating, and the contacts that I made from them were priceless. It was a glimpse into another world that I would never have seen on television. It actually made me think of changing careers and going into law enforcement but when I looked into it further I found that I needed way more science education than I'd ever wanted to get and that I'd have to want to deal with evidence. Blood and guts. I decided to stay in the realm of technical communication. It was a much dryer, cleaner world.

Another thing that I did as part of my book research involved touring crime labs. Many of them have tours that are open to the public in case you'd like the experience for yourself. I was fortunate that one of my course instructors was high up in the Washington State crime lab and I got private tours of the Marysville lab and also the San Diego Police crime lab. An odd coincidence was that the director of the San Diego lab happened to be the guy who got teeth impressions from Ted Bundy when he was arrested in the Chi Omega killings. He kept one of the impressions and it sits on a file cabinet in his office to this day.

This seems to be a weird interest, but I've been comforted by the fact that we now have a tremendous selection of true and fictional crime solving series on television. I am not alone in my fixation with crime. Maybe I have a morbid interest because I was victimized several times and know the horror of being captured and unable to do anything about it.

When I was four years old, my babysitter, Chucky (yes, really), had a friend, Junior, who was seventeen who saw me in my front yard and somehow convinced me to walk off with him into the woods near our house. My parents found me yelling at him to leave me alone, and I was crying. He'd been trying to get my clothes off. I don't recall much about that day except that my dog was the one who led my parents to me and he was barking and jumping on me. I think we all know what would have happened if I hadn't been found in time.

I was kidnapped at gun point when I was seventeen and was held for approximately 20 hours before he let me go. I thought I would be killed the entire time he held me and was relieved when he let me out of his car in northern California. He was never caught.

Terror recedes in time, but the distrust of other people never completely goes away. It has turned me into a very careful person and made me experience the world of the unpleasant. I can't feel the joy of life and living a new day without knowing what might happen. That's the real crime—stealing away my innocence.

Manspeak

I learned about sex from my brothers. Not the act, just the words to describe it. Did you think I meant something else? They would use euphemisms for sex. Words like screw, nail, and bone took on new meanings. My brothers were all younger, yet they seemed to know about all this stuff that I did not have a clue about. The world of guy talk was an interesting world that I could never penetrate, but the occasional glimpses I got through the brothers were fascinating and I mostly responded in disbelief. At the time I thought they were making this stuff up; but now I have a love of language and all of its meanings and I may have gotten it from these puzzling conversations.

I'd hear a word from them and would be shocked at what they said it meant, so I'd go to my mother and ask her. Of course this blew my mother's mind and she would look at me as if I were crazy before telling me that the brothers were right.

We didn't have a very comprehensive sex education class at my school. I never got the idea that people actually connected with each other during sex. They discussed body parts and reproduction, but just forgot to mention where tab A is inserted into slot B. Somehow the idea of connection was not communicated in class at all.

It's funny how years later I still notice that boy talk became man talk and there is still a difference in the way we talk about sex. Yet, if you look at the topics in women's magazines, sex is a prominent topic.

Adventures with Ambien and Other Stories

Glamour Magazine always advertises at least one article on "How to Please your Man" or "Ten Ways to Make Him Love You". Women's Health has a full section full of articles on sex. Men want sex and women want sex. Both sides say they want relationships. Yet is seems like so few of us are happy about the sex we're having or not having. So for all the years I've been alive, sex continues to be a huge motivator; and yet no one seems to be getting enough of it.

I belong to an organization where people state what it is they want in life and so often, both men and women want to find a mate. They express it as a top priority, yet they don't look at the people around them as being "mate" material. They complain they can never find anyone when there are lonely people surrounding them.

Women tend to look at a man and try to fit them into a relationship from the very beginning, sort of like trying to dress Barbie's boyfriend Ken in his tuxedo. With each date, the tuxedo fits better or not at all. But we tend to go into a new relationship hopeful that it will be the one.

Men that I've talked to about this generally confess that their initial attraction is sexual. They're thinking how to get laid and then if things work out in other ways they are happy. Not that they don't want a relationship to begin with, but it just isn't the first thing they focus on.

When I met my husband, I had an initial very physical reaction to him. My knees buckled slightly and I got very red in the face. At the time, I was aware of the reaction but didn't quite understand it. I didn't start dating him until I'd known him for several months.

So here's what I wonder. If men are still speaking man speak, and women want a romantic mate, did we somehow grow up and still not figure out how to insert tab A into slot B on a mental or emotional level? If we open our minds, can we fall in love with someone we don't initially see as mate material? Is it all in our heads? Is it in our hearts? Or is it something chemical in our loins? I don't know the answer but I am actively looking into the question.

I'm Not Crazy, Just Creative

I don't know why this has happened, but in my life I've been told I am crazy or that I am overly sensitive. Usually men are the ones who say this and they usually say it when I say I want to do more with my life than I've been doing. Brothers, fathers, and boyfriends have all said this in one way or another at some time in my life. I have always felt I had something more to contribute, someplace else to go, and expectations for myself that I guess were outside their expectations or comfort zone. This may happen because I don't include those men in my dreams, but I don't really know how to. They just fit in if they stay and if they don't they go. I don't know. But I have decided not to listen to them, and that's why I am writing this book.

It started when I was young. I came from a very dysfunctional family; rules changed according to the mood of my parents, normal was a concept and not even an ideal, and chaos reigned. I had seven younger brothers and was the only girl. Men were put on a pedestal and women were supposed to serve them which meant that I had an awful lot of chores and responsibility at a young age. My mother has since apologized for this attitude but that's how it was when I was growing up.

In defense of my parents, my mother lived in an adoption facility or group home for much of her life and my father was in and out of foster care until he ran away and lived on the streets until he was seventeen when he lied about his age and went into the Army. So they had no clue about normal family life. It took me years to understand their circumstances and not blame them for our lack of consistency, but I do know that now.

I thank God my parents moved us from New Jersey to California when I was ten and I don't have one of those awful accents that many fine New Jersey

Lin Laurie

natives are sporting. Thank you for making sure I didn't turn into Snookie from Jersey Shores, or someone like that. Thank you so much!!!

I'm not sure if I just marched to the beat of a different drummer through genetics or if I just grew up that way because our family was so weird, however, whatever the reason, I was always different from my family. When I was 14, I was reading a book about a girl who was adopted and hadn't been told. I recall looking at my brothers; they were all blondes with blue eyes, and me with my long, auburn hair and green eyes just did not look like them. I felt like an alien in my own house and asked my mother.

"Was I adopted?" I only asked as I was being bratty.

"Yes." My mother was very succinct.

"You aren't my mother?" I was now alarmed and shocked.

"Your father adopted you when you were two." She said.

"He isn't my dad?" I was now alarmed.

"Just stop it. He is your father and you're being overly sensitive."

It's funny about a word. The word adoption didn't exist in our family until I brought it in the door by asking the question. Now, in less than a minute I created a family that now looked at relatedness in a whole new way. Before, it was something we all took for granted.

That was how I found out I really didn't belong to this house of misfits. But then again, she was my mother and they were my half-brothers. We weren't raised that way and it never came up as an issue, but in the moment, my world was rocked and I never again felt sure of anything. After all, there might be secrets out there that I didn't know about and might unwittingly unearth.

Later in life I found out I was very fortunate in many ways. We had a relatively secure life compared to many of my friends, no one went to a group home, we were all loved, no one starved, and no one was abused. Well, in those days verbal abuse wasn't counted. We had to be tough enough to handle that kind of thing.

My parents had done a wonderful job of taking the issues they'd faced as children and protected us from them but substituting other ones into our lives. But instead, we faced a lack of boundaries, insecurities, and self-doubt. Many of my brothers have had addiction issues. I stuffed my feelings with food so as not to experience the emotional pain of being different. This isn't a statement about my parents; they did the best they could and as I said, it was so much better than a lot of other people I know.

The next time you tell someone in some way that their feelings don't count or aren't valid, remember that this type of pain is the equivalent of putting weed killer on a weed. It subtly kills off the weed or causes the emotional death of the roots of our feelings. Don't discount—instead promote the differences in all of us and channel them into helping us find something in ourselves to be proud of.

At the age of twenty-five I quit my job as a systems analyst and started my own company. I bought my first house, a fancy sports car, and lots of other material crap, and had a fair amount of success doing my own thing. When I first told my parents that I had quit a great paying job, they truly believed only a crazy person would quit a steady job to have no job of their own and it took a long time to convince them that it was working out.

I recognized early in life that I had restless nature for the conventional and I wanted more than most people seemed to very early in my life. It isn't crazy to dream of a better life for yourself if you also believe in the possibility of it happening and you can put forth the actions to achieve it.

Adventures with Ambien and Other Stories

Most of us don't dare to dream. We don't know how to dream and then create a life based on that dream. We don't think we are worthy of reaching for the great, big, never on sale, extra-large size, juicy with feelings, fulfilling kind of life. We aren't pretty enough or thin enough for the perfect relationship. We aren't smart enough, clever enough, brave enough to dare to believe we can have anything more than we've already got.

We each need to change that opinion of ourselves and realize we are deserving of all of that and more. Then we can convince others of our convictions and possibilities.

From the experiences I had growing up, I fought feeling worthless and countered it by feeling I was able to achieve a lot in life as long as it was something I did alone.

I am hopeful that I will meet the perfect guy and have a great life as I shed the things that stop me. Maybe that's optimistic but I have always been one and will continue on that track. Since I started this book, I've accomplished the following:

- Joined a program to become a seminar leader.
- Completed this book.
- Become a part-time motivating speaker for a local non-profit organization.
- Started an outline for a reality TV show.

Lin Laurie

- Reconciled with family and friends where I had issues.
- Taken steps to reconcile a couple of work-related relationships that I wish had turned out differently.
- Reduced my reliance on Ambien by 50% and am sleeping well.
- Started an exercise and weight-loss program and have started doing 5Ks and have friends who support me in my program.
- Joined Weight Watchers and started losing weight. To date my weight loss is small but my medical test scores are much better and I can see I am slowly making progress. I am much more active and I feel so much better now.
- Taken the entire curriculum for living at Landmark Education.

I am on fire and I plan to keep on going because I want to live an unstoppable life!

Epilog

I started to do some personal development work in the eighties and then strayed away from that work until last year. I am a proud Landmark Forum graduate and am in the process of become a course introduction leader because I so strongly believe in the work of Landmark Education. It is in doing this work that I found the strength and confidence to write this book. I've also been developing skills in motivating others by word and by deed. I am finding my way by using their program as a structure for working my life and while it isn't always easy, I love the results of the work. If you don't know about Landmark Education, I encourage you to go to <http://www.landmarkeducation.com/> and view the online video for Introduction to the Landmark Forum. You'll be glad you did.

Lin Laurie

Courtesy of Jennifer Gorman

About the Author

Lin Laurie currently lives in San Diego, California and works as an instructional designer and trainer as she transforms her career into that of a writer and lecturer. She continues to write and is currently working on her second book, a story about six inmates about to be released from prison and their adventures while still confined in a job reentry program. She continues to be an advocate for Landmark Education and is currently in training to be a Forum introduction leader.